Country Home®
Collection

Country Home

Editor in Chief: Jean LemMon
Executive Editor: Ann Omvig Maine
Art Director: Peggy A. Fisher

Senior Editor: Beverly Hawkins
Copy Chief/Production Editor: Angela K. Renkoski
Interior Design Director: Candace Ord Manroe
Interior Designer: Joseph Boehm
Building Editor: Steve Cooper
Food and Tabletop Editor: Lisa Kingsley
Antiques and Garden Editor: Linda Joan Smith
Assistant Art Directors: Sue Mattes, Shelley Caldwell
Administrative Assistant: Becky A. Brame
Art Business Clerk: Jacalyn M. Mason
Editorial Trainee: Lisa C. Jones

Publisher: Terry McIntyre

MEREDITH DESIGN GROUP
Vice President/Editorial Director: Dorothy Kalins
Vice President/Publishing Director: Stephen R. Burzon
Editorial Services Director: Charla Lawhon

President/Magazine Group: William T. Kerr

BETTER HOMES AND GARDENS ₨ BOOKS
President, Book Group: Joseph J. Ward
Vice President and Editorial Director: Elizabeth P. Rice
Vice President, Retail Marketing: Jamie L. Martin
Vice President, Book Clubs: Richard L. Rundall

COUNTRY HOME ₨ COLLECTION
Editor: Jean LemMon
Project Editor: Marsha Jahns
Graphic Designer: Mary Schlueter Bendgen
Electronic Text Processor: Paula Forest

Contents

Homes are more than wood, stone, brick, and glass. I've always felt that homes have personalities and, like people, flourish when  they're loved or suffer when they're neglected. And they all have stories to tell. The 22 homes featured in this COUNTRY HOME. COLLECTION are an anthology of happy-ending stories—tales of caring, remodeling, restoring, planning, and building. Join me as we visit favorite Country Home houses and gardens chosen from our 1991 issues. Meet the people who love these homes and believe, as I do, that a home is more than an amalgamation of building products.

Jean Lemmon

February

Building the Country House

THE NEW-FASHIONED FARMHOUSE

With touches of the past, *Country Home*® editors have reshaped the traditional American farmhouse to serve family life-styles into the future.

By Steve Cooper. Interior Design by Joseph Boehm. Produced with Ann Omvig Maine and Peggy A. Fisher

Like an engrossing book or a riveting movie, a successful house begins with an easily stated idea, a high concept, a compelling hook.

When editors at *Country Home®* magazine decided to build in the Hamptons region of New York's Long Island, the concept was concise: Take the familiar family farmhouse and breathe freshness into its ageless, friendly style.

American farm dwellings dating to the mid-19th century were always shelters that soothed and embraced. They weren't castles. They were refuges where handwork spoke of the elegance of simplicity.

Latter-day stylists may strive for architecture that resonates with the soul. They need look no further for inspiration than crisp, workaday farmhouses dotting the landscape from the potato fields of Long Island to the vineyards of the California coast.

Country Home's winsome interpretation of this form can also serve to inspire building projects.

Editor Jean LemMon says, "This is the familiar family farmhouse but with a new, fresh twist. Carefully chosen details from the past add

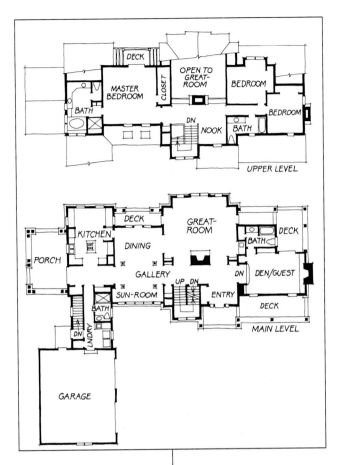

character to contemporary spaces and lofty rooms."

At about 3,200 square feet, the house welcomes with a relaxed farmhouse attitude. Contemporary efficiency and performance haven't been forgotten, however. The folksy and the innovative combine to celebrate the past yet prepare for the future.

Among the highlights

Left: *The lofty great-room becomes intimate with a tight but never cramped arrangement of furnishings.* Below: *A three-point, front door lock adds security.*

THE NEW-FASHIONED
FARMHOUSE

in our New-Fashioned Farmhouse are such touches as:

- A paneled oak front door that evokes a quality of craftsmanship coveted for generations. This one features the security and energy savings of a three-point lock set.
- Faultless 5-inch-wide oak floors.
- A central fireplace as a focal point in a lofty great-room. This room blends smoothly with an adjacent dining room, which is distinguished by its air of informality.
- Kitchen design that allows for such diverse elements as a plate rail, wainscoting, and an array of major appliances fitted with birch panels matching the cabinets.
- Three upstairs bedrooms, including a master bedroom suite. A downstairs room with full bath could be another bedroom, study, or den.
- Radiant heating that utilizes both underfloor tubing and radiators in baseboards and on walls.
- A back porch with motorized awnings.
- A pondlike swimming pool. A miniature waterfall adds a bit of whimsy.

The journey from rough lot to completed farmhouse was a group effort—from

the first architectural drawings to the brick-by-brick placement of driveway paving stones. It carries the magazine staff's imprint, but also that of a small army of talented home builders.

The genesis of the New-Fashioned Farmhouse goes back to spring 1989. Jim McGinniss, a Sag Harbor, New York, real estate developer, approached *Country Home* about putting the magazine's next project home on a wooded Long Island lot.

"It was like so many things. Everyone told me I was crazy to even approach a national

Left: *The floor plan has a contemporary feel with the dining room opening into the living room.*
Above: *A gallery separates sunroom and dining room.*
Below: *Developers Anthony and Dorothy Pintauro are seated. Standing are development coordinator Jim McGinniss, right, and builder Robert Pintauro.*

THE NEW-FASHIONED
FARMHOUSE

Right: *A cooktop island allows plenty of work space.*
Above: *Plain, wide window trim, wainscoting, and a plate rail lends authenticity to the farmhouse atmosphere.*
Below: *Small appliances are in easy reach and they are also easily hidden by tambour doors in cabinets.*

magazine with an idea. But you can't listen to all those people telling you what won't work. Look at the finished product. The house has worked beyond all expectations," Jim says.

He coordinated the home's development for Wind Chimes, Inc., which is owned by Anthony and Dorothy Pintauro, of Garden City, New York. It was built by Robert Pintauro, of Sagg Farms Custom Builders.

From the outset, farm-style architecture seemed an appropriate choice because of Long Island's rich agricultural heritage. Certainly, the island

retains its other rich reputation as a seashore playground for the wealthy, but vegetable fields still green the island's interior and roadside stands still sell the pick of local produce.

Designing the project was architect Kate Schwennsen, of Bloodgood, Sharp, Snider Architects & Planners, Inc., in Des Moines. After meeting with editors to discuss the farmhouse concept, her first step was to research the architectural history of Long Island and farm dwellings in general.

"I tried to get a feel for what a farmhouse would have been like in about 1850. I didn't want to duplicate that house exactly. But I wanted someone who sees this house for the first time to easily recognize where the inspiration for the style came from," Kate says.

Typically, farmhouses were built in segments. They appeared to be products of evolution rather than detailed master plans.

When a farm family was young and small, a suitably compact first dwelling would suffice. As the family grew, so did the house—with newer sections added to each side

THE NEW-FASHIONED FARMHOUSE

of the original structure. Kate's design reflects this look and continues the theme with covered porches, cross gables, a rear dormer, and multiple-pane windows.

"Most farmhouses are comfortable, inviting places. Informal. A spot where visitors are welcome and instantly feel at home," the architect says.

Successfully creating this atmosphere resulted from staying true to the original concept. It was a quality of ease sought by Jean from the start.

"Formal, fancy, and fussy don't apply here. Rather, these are warm spaces that invite you to put your feet up and relax," the editor says.

The magazine's interior designer, Joseph Boehm, performed a balancing act. On one side, he had a farmhouse flavor to express. On the other, the house had to exude an air of sophistication in keeping with its trendsetting neighborhood.

Joe says, "The decor itself is low-key and charming. We've created an unpretentious scheme as opposed to something high end.

"For instance, the fabrics have a farmhouse flavor with cottons and

linens instead of a rich silk or damask. We wanted to subtly enhance that quality of simplicity."

To fill the great-room, he chose sizable furnishings covered with geometric-pattern fabrics. The interior might easily have been made too cutesy if smothered with calicos and small-scale prints.

The color palette in most rooms was soothing combinations of white,

Left: *The den becomes a study in monochromatic hues. A mantel salvaged from an old home perfectly blends with the farmhouse character. The hearth has the appearance of imported marble, but it's plywood painted by John Heldreth with latex and coats of linseed oil.*
Above: *The den's bathroom.*

□ □ □

THE NEW-FASHIONED FARMHOUSE

Right: *A cedar-plank ceiling and wood floor painted in checkerboard pattern keep the master bedroom from becoming too citified. The balcony overlooks the backyard pool.* Above: *The spacious master bathroom includes a whirlpool, a shower lined with faux-stone countertop material, and two sinks. There's also a towel-warming radiator mounted next to the bath.*

□ □ □

blue, and yellow.

"I've chosen a provincial European color scheme, and the colors offset one another nicely. Because they are primary colors, they give rooms a farmhouse look," Joe says.

This is best seen in the kitchen eating area. Here, simple forms—wood trim, square floor tile, and ladder-back chairs—take on visual appeal when splashed with a bold blue.

Throughout the house, elements have been chosen because they echo the farm dwelling of the past without hampering contemporary comfort.

For instance, the study seems to have emerged

from another era with its aged pine mantel, wainscoting, and stenciled floor. The mantel is genuine, having come from an architectural salvage emporium. The wainscoting can be purchased at home centers and installs in minutes.

Floor stenciling is also appropriate to a farmhouse. Exquisite rugs may have been beyond the means of a plowman, but paint was always cheap.

John Heldreth, of Faux Finishing, stippled on floor patterns using stencils created by Adele Bishop and Cile Lord. He also fashioned a faux-marble hearth and a checkerboard-pattern bedroom floor.

In two upstairs bedrooms, John gave walls subtle paint effects with distressing techniques called ragging and bagging. In both instances, he started with an undercoat of one color. Then, he achieved a dappled finish with a second color applied either with a piece of cloth or a paper bag.

The blue master bedroom was bagged—a dark latex coat over a light undercoat. A cloudy pink bedroom was ragged— light over dark.

"It's much easier to do

THE NEW-FASHIONED FARMHOUSE

Right: *A child's room has been finished in a soft, romantic distressed pink. Wide baseboards are actually heating radiators. The pine armoire and sleigh bed are reproductions licensed by the Museum of American Folk Art.* Above: *This nook at the top of the stairs is an ideal spot for reading, knitting, or other quiet pursuits.*

□ □ □

the ragging. With the paper bag, there's always a tendency for it to tear after you wad it up and dip it in a big old paint bucket," John says.

While the faux painter was busy with his calming colors and stately stencils, the heart of the farmhouse—the kitchen—was not overlooked. Designed by the magazine's managing editor, Ann Omvig Maine, it appears as tasty as ripe, ready-to-pick fruit.

Working convenience was uppermost in mind. Plentiful cabinets are equipped for every storage task. Durability and elegance make faux-stone

countertops a favored surface with designers.

Easy preparation begins with a well-equipped kitchen. Appliances include two undercounter ovens, an island cooktop with downdraft venting, two refrigerator/freezers (one on the cooking side of the island, the other a step away from the dining room), and a wine cooler with a glass door.

Neutral kitchen colors are enlivened with blue highlights on both woodwork and floor tiles.

"These kind of simple details—like the blue plate rail—add charm and interesting character so often found lacking in today's houses," Joe says.

Other valuable garnishes can be seen just outside the kitchen on the covered back porch. A relatively ordinary platform is given a romantic feel with the addition of wicker furnishings, a ceiling fan, and awnings that can be extended or retracted at the flip of a switch. These canvas coverings not only increase shade on bright days, but they add spice to conservative architecture.

Less noticeable, but worth noting, are the use of durable, quality products. This includes such items as double-pane

THE NEW-FASHIONED
FARMHOUSE

Right: *For photography, pool fencing was removed. However, New York law and safety requires fencing around a finished pool.*
Above: *Colorful, motorized awnings add to the cool.*
Below: *From right, Joseph Boehm, Kate Schwennsen, and Steve Cooper.*

insulating windows, high-performance paints, and a urethane-rubber compound for a balcony floor exposed to harsh weather.

Another vital but unobtrusive component that makes the house an inviting place to be is the radiant heating system utilizing underfloor pipes and radiators.

Warmth is generated by water fired in a basement heating unit and pumped silently throughout the house. In tiled areas, such as the kitchen, flexible tubing has been snaked between the subfloor and the walking surface. Hot water heats the tiles, which then heats the

room. Where wood floors have been installed, the water flows through inconspicuous baseboard and wall radiators. The system heats evenly; plus, toes stay warm.

When the project was complete last August, builder Robert Pintauro paid tribute to the crew.

"A house like this generally takes fourteen months to build from the time we lay the foundation. But we made it in less than eight months. It was a great effort by my crew and all the subcontractors working together," Robert says.

The builder learned some tricks, too, he says.

"On future houses I'll use things like the master bedroom closet carousel. Joe showed me what wallpaper can do to add color. The porch awning is a strong focal point. Who could improve on the driveway or the front door or the wainscoting? The list goes on," he says.

Indeed, it does. These choices, and many more, spring from the same source—the original concept of the house. That was the ultimate arbiter of taste in shaping the look and feel of the New-Fashioned Farmhouse.□

THE NEW-FASHIONED FARMHOUSE

VACATION
Vernacular

Tom and Polly Minick needed an escape from the daily routine. What better than a log cabin on an island? Now it's their full-time home during the warm seasons.

By Steve Cooper
Produced with Jean LemMon

A cabin in the woods. The retreat of Tom and Polly Minick perfectly captures all the nuance packed into that lovely-sounding phrase.

Peace. Relaxation. Serenity. It's the way things were meant to be; the way things are on Lake Huron's Drummond Island in Michigan's northern reaches.

Even in winter, isolated by imposing billows of snow, the allure of this cabin in the woods is strong. Who cares if the copper roof is hidden beneath downy white and

Canada is a five-mile snowmobile ride across a frozen Great Lake?

"If you can't find me, this is where I am. I can sit here by the fireplace and unwind. There's no place else like it," Polly says.

"It's the kind of log cabin you dream about. We were very fortunate," Tom says.

But before the mid-1980s, the Minicks had little time for retreats. Tom was sheriff of Washtenaw County, serving the region around Ann Arbor, Michigan. Also, the Minicks spent most weekends with three sons—Jeff, John, and Jim—who pursued athletics from elementary school through college.

In 1984, however, Tom made a dramatic switch. He resigned after he was named a vice president at Domino's Pizza. Still working and living in Ann Arbor, one of his earliest tasks was to negotiate purchase of Drummond Island property for the corporation.

"It wasn't what I expected to be

Opposite: *Rustic bent-twig furniture accents a screened back porch. The view includes a pond and frequent visits from island deer.*
Above: *The copper-roofed log cabin of Tom and Polly Minick.*

Photographs: Jim Hedrich, Hedrich-Blessing; Minicks' portrait, Jim Kelley

doing, but here I was. I'd never been to Drummond Island, and on my first trip, I was helping to buy part of it for Domino's," he said.

Within a few months, the couple began planning their own retreat.

"Before I left law enforcement, I didn't have time to think about a place in the woods," Tom says.

Nor did Polly. For her, it was more a matter of temperament than a lack of time for such daydreaming. Despite her present enjoyment of island life, she's not a leisurely person. Play is work, and she feels compelled to earn her bit of rest.

"I'm a real type-A personality. It's taken me a while to learn how to relax. Even surrounded by all this natural beauty, I've got to keep busy," she says.

If she isn't in the hunt for a bargain in an antiques store, her hands are nimbly hooking rugs of her design. Her days have always been full to overflowing.

Back when Tom went to work for Domino's, so did Polly. She organizes special projects for business founder Tom Monaghan. On the island, she has also been a buyer for a small antiques shop and has helped decorate the corporate lodge.

"One day I was very involved in Ann Arbor. It seemed like the next day, I was working for Domino's and, then, coming to the island every chance I got. It all happened so fast," Polly says.

The cabin happened fast, too. It was built on a secluded spot away from the corporate retreat's center. It's a clearing ringed by maples, where one can often watch deer, an occasional bear, or other wildlife sunning themselves.

"We always talked about a log cabin in the woods, but we never really expected to get one. It's amazing how these things have evolved," Tom says.

Builder Bob Van Slot, an island resident, began selecting towering red pines needed for the cabin in late 1985. Tom joined Van Slot in the search for timber and later helped erect walls of log.

"These were huge trees—some had to be thirty-five feet high—and it was a great pleasure helping Bob with the work. Hard work, but great fun and very therapeutic," Tom says.

Before it was built at the site, the home's shell was erected at the island mill, where logs were prepared. Every log was cleaned of bark, notched, and numbered before the cabin was assembled and disassembled. Walls were stacked much like a child's toy log set.

The result is exactly what the couple wanted. It's rustic, charming, and the interior is a mix of openness and toasty, get-close coziness. The main living area soars—the living room, dining area, and kitchen are a single space open to the sleeping loft

Above: *Tom and Polly Minick.*
Left: *Drummond Islander Bob Van Slot built the dwelling using red pines from surrounding forest. The trees were at least 22 inches thick and up to 35 feet long. Bill Robinson used locally quarried stone to build the fireplace. Polly found the fish on the mantel in an Ohio craft shop.*

VACATION
Vernacular

and log rafters above. The primary downstairs bedroom promises intimacy with its fireplace of locally quarried stone, easy-reach ceiling, and simplicity.

All this in a cabin that is not quite 40 feet square.

"My husband and I were very active in the design of the house. We drew out the floor plan pretty much the way it is," Polly says.

Originally, the cabin's roof was to have been cedar shakes, which Tom was making by slavishly splitting timbers with hand tools. Plans changed, however, and the four private residences at the 1,800-acre resort were fitted with copper roofs.

"We wound up using my shakes under the roof overhangs, so my labor wasn't in vain," Tom says.

Little more than half a year after construction began, the cabin was ready for the couple to move in during the summer of 1986.

"You must say that our builder was really an artist. He did a

masterful job working with the logs and making the cabin exactly what we had in mind. In fact, the logs fit together so well, when we finally put in chinking it was more for looks than anything else," Polly says.

After the cabin was completed, it was christened with the crash of a champagne bottle.

When the Minicks first moved in, they exclusively used the main downstairs bedroom. As inviting as the sleeping loft was, Polly couldn't find a bed properly balancing the room's feeling of rough-hewn elegance. Then she saw a bed by New York woodcrafter Ken Heitz, who was featured in *Country Home*® magazine's June 1989 issue.

Opposites attract in this bedroom. Ruffles, floral prints, and softly colored linens are counterpoints to raw cabin timbers and the white birch of the bedposts.

"Our only problem with the bed was getting it into the loft. We had to disconnect the railings before we

had enough room to lift it up there," Polly says.

For many visitors, the favorite spot to lounge will be the screened porch across the rear of the house. Much like the cabin, the furniture here is rustic and heavy. Cushions are deep and offer a pleasant vantage point for observing deer as they drink from Lake Marge, a tranquil pond.

"Just last night, I was sitting there when a mother deer and three fawns walked by. That was unusual—to see three fawns," Tom says.

Opposite: *Separate undercounter freezer and refrigerator units make for a fully equipped compact kitchen. The cast-iron wood stove helps heat the cabin and cook meals on wintry nights. A small guest bedroom can be seen through the doorway and the sleeping loft is above.*
Above: *The living room and dining area are a single open space continuing into the kitchen. Braided rugs define the spaces.*

VACATION Vernacular

Such occurrences have changed the way Tom thinks about day-to-day living. He likes the slower pace.

"It took me a while after twenty-three years in law enforcement, but I gradually began to have less tolerance for certain elements of city life—the traffic, the pollution, the crime, people always in a rush. All that is quite a contrast to laid-back island living," he says.

When the cabin was first built, the Minicks island-hopped at least once a month from their home in Ann Arbor, where the pizza company's international headquarters is located. Polly's schedule allowed her to spend more time on the island than Tom. Fortunately, he holds a pilot's license, which enabled him to make the hour-plus flight frequently.

A year ago they were able to increase their time on the island considerably when Tom was named president of the company retreat. A hotel and golf course open to the public have been added.

Though they still maintain an Ann Arbor home, the Minicks are island residents during warmer months. Polly couldn't be happier.

"I love the dress code of the island: There isn't one. When my husband was working at headquarters, he was always in a business suit. But up here, it's more casual. It's more like him," she says.

The move has also opened new avenues for Polly. In addition to her decorating and the antiques store, she has taken up golf.

"A year ago if you'd told me I'd be out on the golf course, I'd have said you were crazy. But I'm out there and I love it," she says.

Surprisingly, the transformation of the cabin from an occasional getaway into long-term shelter required only small adjustments. The primary additions were a stone patio off the screened rear porch and a microwave oven.

"We really didn't need to do much. The cabin was almost perfect for the

two of us the way it was," Polly says.

The only time it becomes cramped is during a family reunion every Thanksgiving. That's when the Minicks' three sons make their annual trek home.

Polly says: "At first it was hard to think of this as home. Because I like to be on the go so much, all the quiet up here took some getting used to.

"But, you know, once you get out here among the trees and the clean air and the peacefulness, it does grow on you. We're lucky to have our cabin in the woods." □

Opposite: *The white-birch four-poster standing as the centerpiece of the sleeping loft was crafted by Adirondack Mountain woodworker Ken Heitz (whose rustic furniture was featured in* Country Home® *magazine's June 1989 issue).*
Above: *With its low ceiling and fireplace, this main-floor bedroom is inviting during crisp nights both winter and summer.*

Bedroom linens: Ralph Lauren Home Collection

29

Although the 20th century and streams of tourists have brought many changes to this small New Mexico town, an air of tranquillity reminiscent of Spanish colonial days still lingers.

The narrow streets bustle with modern-day commerce. Beyond the high adobe walls, however, another Santa Fe abides. Fountains splash and gurgle in the dry mountain air, 200-year-old adobe dwellings soak up the desert sun, and shaded courtyards offer cool respite from the dusty streets.

The lush garden of Dian and Donald Malouf is cloistered in one such protected spot, only inches from a busy and arid downtown street. A refreshing oasis, the garden overflows with an abundance of old-fashioned perennials, boldly colored annuals, folksy pots, sculptures, and water-polished river rocks.

"I call it southwestern Zen with a mixture of English," says Dian, the garden's creator. "The succulents are southwestern, the rocks are Zen, and the rest is English."

When the Maloufs bought their small weekend house in Santa Fe eight years ago, Dian had little interest in gardening.

"We hired a few gardeners, but it just was never what I wanted," she says. "Finally, I just decided to do it myself."

Opposite *and* above: *Donald and Dian Malouf's courtyard is a well-used extension of their tiny weekend hideaway. In traditional style, each of their home's three rooms has a door that opens onto the lushly planted space. Whimsical flea-market finds help Dian add her personal touch to plantings. When the doors are left ajar on Santa Fe's summer days, the garden serves as another room of the house.*

Top: *Dian Malouf—jewelry designer, store owner, and author—uses her garden as yet another place to express her creativity. Here, she reclines on pillows made by Jean Stitt, a close friend.*

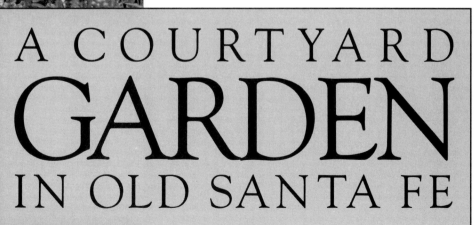

A COURTYARD
GARDEN
IN OLD SANTA FE

By Linda Joan Smith
Produced by Amy Muzzy Malin

Photographs: Jenifer Jordan.

Though she approached the project with a good deal of naïveté ("The only thing I knew about gardening was that tall things have to go in the back," she says), the resulting medley of elements is far from the work of a novice. The concrete walkways and brick patio area are embraced by beds and potted plants that bloom profusely, filling the courtyard with color throughout Santa Fe's short growing season.

According to Dian, Santa Fe gardeners commonly mix many types of plants in a single pot, from lobelia and petunias to coreopsis, zinnias, and sweet William. She has wholeheartedly adopted the local custom, which meshes well with her own eclectic leanings.

Extending the tradition from container plantings to her garden beds, Dian mixes her floral hues and types with abandon. The soft greens and grays of lavender and dusty miller are backed by cool plumes of delphinium and larkspur, black-eyed Susans, and sunny heads of yarrow. Compact sweet alyssum and snapdragons rub shoulders with pink ageratum and golden marigolds, while heavy-headed zinnias and a rainbow of petunias fill in the gaps between diminutive and stately plants.

Opposite *and* left: *A rustic twig settee and matching chair, purchased from a roadside stand, seem at home in their Santa Fe surroundings. Dian softened both pieces with pillows and cushions that echo the garden's rich hues. The twig table was a flea-market purchase and moves easily from inside when needed.*

Below: *The whimsical stone lamb reclining in a shaded garden corner was a Christmas gift from Donald to Dian.*

A COURTYARD
GARDEN
IN OLD SANTA FE

"My garden has evolved," says Dian. "I never have a plan for anything, so it just happened."

The plants thrive with this casual approach, encouraged by dependable sunshine, afternoon thundershowers, and cool Santa Fe nights. "The climate is so wonderful here that you can toss seeds anywhere and they will grow," Dian says.

Though the brilliant blooms and lush greenery delight the senses, other elements conspire to bring a bit of Santa Fe magic to this protected garden spot. A trellised entrance, built by the previous owners, was intended for hanging potted flowers, but Dian keeps it unadorned to show off its bold southwestern design. Rather than relying on traditional clay pots for all of her container plantings, Dian grows some of her flowers in colorful flea-market and yard-sale finds: a metate, painted Mexican gourds, an old wooden ice-cream freezer. A variety of sculptures nestled in the garden beds adds additional folk art charm.

Never one to rest on her laurels, Dian continually regroups her potted plants, sculptures, and other garden elements to create an ever-changing scene as colorful and entertaining as the historic town around the Maloufs' home. "It's rewarding to the soul and spirit," she says. □

A COURTYARD
GARDEN
IN OLD SANTA FE

RESTORED WITH

Realism

The restoration of an early Maine cottage keeps both the period and practicality in mind.

By Candace Ord Manroe.
Produced by Ann Omvig Maine

Beginning with the symmetry of its classic Cape Cod architecture, the restored circa-1804 North Brooklin, Maine, cottage of John and Beth Hikade is an adroit balancing act.

Period authenticity is valued but not precious; antiques are collected but without compulsion. As a restoration, the home is tempered by reality—not so purist that an occasional liberty isn't taken here and there for the sake of practicality.

In straying neither too far toward a blithe disregard for the past nor toward a slavish dependence on it, the home succeeds by affording optimum comfort for Beth, John, and their two children, Andrew, 6, and Timothy, 8.

"The idea was to renovate and make the house usable in the modern life but keep it as original as possible," says John. "Obviously, there has to be a little give-and-take in that process."

Unlike many homeowners, John had no trouble translating his goals into action when it

Above: John and Beth Hikade and sons Timothy, 8, and Andrew, 6, take a hands-on approach to history in their vintage 1804 Cape Cod cottage, left, that John restored. Top: Family dog Tess romps in front of a shingled outbuilding John returned to its original purpose, crafting his histori-cally influenced origi-nal furniture designs.

Realism

came work time. He circumvented potential communication problems altogether by doing most of the restoration himself.

Two things ensured his success: his prior experience in restoration work while living on Martha's Vineyard, where he and Beth met, and the surprisingly sound condition of the home.

"When we bought it in 1980, it had been in one family for a very long time. Apparently the people in that family didn't have many children because the house was in remarkably good shape," explains John.

"It wasn't all beat up as houses often are when there are big families involved. It hadn't been modernized by anyone in the past. It did have some very basic wiring and plumbing in it, but nobody had done anything too radical to it," adds Beth.

Before moving into the home in the spring, John spent the winter readying it, replacing wiring, plumbing, and siding.

Old wood shingles that covered the facade were paper thin, and a clapboard rear section of the home that apparently had escaped shingling during an

---

Left: *A balance of old and new pervades the living room: The tall case clock is a Shaker reproduction crafted by John, and the Joshua Wilder table clock is an antique.*
Above: *By the living room fireplace, an unusual high-arm chair from the Canadian maritimes features its original paint.*

39

Realism

earlier cosmetic redo had square nails that were rusted and crumbling.

"A friend of ours discovered a very old painting of this house from the late 1800s. It shows a portion of the house unshingled, covered in clapboard, so it seemed appropriate to put clapboard back," John says.

Four courses of shingles covered the roof—two asphalt layers over two cedar-shingle layers. "I stripped the entire roof and replaced whatever boards needed to be replaced and reshingled it," says John. He also rebuilt the center chimney above the fireplaces with special restoration bricks that had been water-struck and then fired in a wood kiln.

Sometimes, the restoration resulted in some unexpected finds. "The original ceiling was falling down, so I helped it along," says John. "Beneath it, I found eight-by-eight timbers that ran a full twenty-six feet. I suspect they were virgin timber when the house was built."

Realizing that exposed beams would have been likely only in a more primitive home of the early

Left *and* top: *Before the completion of John's new kitchen addition (not shown), the keeping room, which now serves primarily as a dining area, had to suffice for the growing family's needs. Filled with family antiques, the room features the original ceiling beams, which were discovered intact during the restoration, as well as flooring found in the attic.* Above: *Early hanging cupboards provide storage space.*

1800s, John decided to fudge on historical accuracy just a little, anyway. To him, the beams simply added too much warmth and charm to the home to be hidden beneath a ceiling, no matter how historically correct it might be.

Similarly, John discovered a solution to replacing the worn-out living room floorboards. "I went up into the attic and found wide, wonderful shiplap boards, two of which were twenty-four feet long and twenty inches wide. I suspected they were the same type that originally covered the living room floor, so down they came," he recalls.

The home is an example of history repeating itself: John builds original design and reproduction furniture in a shop on the property that, coincidentally, originally served as a furniture-making shop.

Like the restoration itself, the furnishings are practical: a mix of family antiques and John's hand-crafted pieces. "The only room off-limits to the boys is the living room," says Beth. "To compensate for that, we gave them a room for play that is the living room's mirror image."

For a restoration, the home is unusually unrestrictive: a well-rounded pleasure for its owners. □

Above: *Tab curtains evoke a period feel in the master bedroom, which includes eclectic pieces such as an antique three-legged English cricket table.*

April

P·E·A·C·E·A·B·L·E
KINGDOM

*Earl Jamison's home and gardens in Bucks County,
Pennsylvania, though new, are a world apart,
linked to the owner's love of the past.*

By Candace Ord Manroe. Produced by Joseph Boehm
and Peggy A. Fisher in cooperation with Waverly

P·E·A·C·E·A·B·L·E
KINGDOM

Architecturally speaking, Earl Jamison doesn't show his age. Rather than taking the usual license to subtract a year here or there, he adds—liberally. Earl's reason is simple: He loves the past. Or, put another way, the older the better.

The new home he shares with "Chee" Hamilton belies its age by appearing as historic as the remainder of Bucks County, Pennsylvania, where it is situated.

The home dominates 40 acres that include woods, fields, and a full 10 acres lavish with gardens that Earl and Chee maintain. Inside, it is filled with antiques and folk art carefully chosen over 25 years of collecting. Grounds and home, together, possess the always-been-there patina and peace of one man's private kingdom.

Although his family didn't make an issue of it while Earl was growing up, the Jamison name was august in his hometown of Jamison, Pennsylvania: It was named after Earl's great-great-great-great-grandfather, who settled there in the 1700s.

"Family history wasn't something that was preached or that was dwelt on, but a strong awareness of it was

Opening page: *Earl Jamison and "Chee" Hamilton take a garden break.*
Left: *In Earl's hypothetical history, the keeping room came first, with low-slung ceilings and log-cabin construction.*
Above: *Wood carvings are favorite collectibles.*
Below: *The dining room floors and beams are old.*

● ● ●

Photographs: interiors and portrait, Judith Watts; exteriors, Julie Maris/Semel, except as noted.

P·E·A·C·E·A·B·L·E
KINGDOM

only natural, growing up in a town with your name," says Earl. "We would visit the museum, and this helped to foster my sense and appreciation of colonial America."

Perhaps unexpectedly, Earl's family did not boast a wealth commensurate with its lineage. "We did not live in the manor house on the hill. Our family was poor. I have a farming background, and I grew up in a simple bungalow," he says.

Ironically, it is certain absences rather than privileges in his early life that Earl credits for producing his now confident and sophisticated taste level—the astute sense of aesthetics that unifies his home. "It required a much stronger quest for me to develop a keen appreciation for detail and beauty, because this wasn't a part of my background," he says.

He earnestly set about cultivating a discerning eye with much the same drive and determination that skyrocketed him to success in commercial development of historic properties.

"One of the things that I do is spend a lot of time looking through books and magazines, searching for architectural ideas that would work in my business," says Earl. "I've been accumulating lots of ideas in my own mind which have a primitive nature to them, so that when it was time to build my own house, all of the research was done and it wasn't difficult to proceed."

"I knew that I wanted a pretty, colonial-type homestead with nice outbuildings and nice grounds," he says. That translated into two springhouses, a barn, chicken house, and garden house come construction time. Earl's concept of his ideal home was so concrete that architects were able to directly transpose his ideas onto paper.

"The house is a very typical reproduction of an early Pennsylvania farmhouse that has been added onto many times over the years," he says.

This hypothetical evolution of the home over the centuries was methodically conceived in Earl's mind,

Left: *Mercer tiles from a local turn-of-the-century shop line the kitchen floor. Even the dishwasher brandishes a colonial spirit, outfitted with a Rufus Porter-style mural.*
Above: *Shirred valances in a colonial-style pattern from Waverly circumscribe the breakfast nook.*
Below: *Even the windowsill's parade of folk art and flowers attests to Earl's passions.*

P·E·A·C·E·A·B·L·E
KINGDOM

then in actuality, in the construction of his new home.

"In my own mind, it started with a small log cabin-type structure, with a large keeping room with a fireplace. As would have been typical, the cabin then was added to with a major stone, two-story structure with a little more formality. Then the kitchen wing was added, and then the library," says Earl.

"Of course, we built it all at once, but that's the explanation for the wonderful rooflines, character, and charm," he adds.

At the same time Earl was honing a decorative eye, he was laying preparatory groundwork for his home through his business. In a real sense, the Jamison home is an extension of that business.

Nearly 30 years ago, he transformed an old chicken farm with its centuries-old buildings into a retail venture that fast became a major tourist and shopping attraction for the tiny town of Lahaska, Pennsylvania. It is also where Earl decided, years later, to build his home.

An old log barn from up-country Pennsylvania was

Left: The colonial spirit is alive in the bedrooms, although in a softer, less primitive vein. The four-poster is an antique, as are the hand-decorated blanket chest, side stand, cradle, and pine chest. The room clearly has a childlike spirit, designed for and used primarily by grandchildren, ages a few months to six years.
Below: *The Waverly florals introduced in the bedroom are repeated in the bathroom, as wallpaper and fabrics.*

● ● ●

P·E·A·C·E·A·B·L·E
KINGDOM

brought to Peddler's Village, along with other vintage buildings accumulated over the years as growth dictated.

Although Earl leases most of the village properties, he owns and operates the flagship enterprise, the Golden Plough Inn, keeping alive a family tradition that's more than 150 years old. One of Earl's ancestors was the town's first innkeeper, running Jamison's Tavern, which now is known as the General Greene Inn.

"My roots are very, very deep in Bucks County, in my love for the land, and in my love for colonial-type architecture," he says.

In scouting for old building materials for Peddler's Village, as well as antiques for the Golden Plough Inn, Earl simultaneously—perhaps subconsciously—amassed a wealth of ideas and preferences for the home he would eventually build for himself.

"In the village, I re-created a nice colonial atmosphere with beautiful landscaping," he says. That same principle guided in building his home.

"In both, I've shown a sensitivity toward architectural detailing and architectural materials, with landscaping that enhances the architecture. Some of the people who are very familiar with the village go to visit my house and say it's just a continuation of the village. It's evident the two were made by the same hand," he concedes.

Just as it is important for Earl to attain historical accuracy in architecture, it is no less important for him to appropriately cushion the home with a soft blanket of gardens and manicured lawns. "I have a deep love for horticulture and a knowledge of it. I could never

Left: Earl makes no apologies for giving equal importance to grounds and home. The 40 acres include a garden house, thousands of flowering plants personally planted by Earl, and 10 acres of lawn.
Above: A gazebo view encompasses a spring-fed pond and outlying meadows.
Bottom: Outbuildings include this springhouse, with its antique red clay roof tiles.

● ● ●

P·E·A·C·E·A·B·L·E
KINGDOM

consider building a building without planning its landscaping at the same time. It's an important part of all that I do," he says.

At his home, and at Peddler's Village, too, he planted every flower himself—"thousands and thousands," he says. There is good reason for that, and Earl is not too modest to admit it. "I do it better than everybody else, and I'm faster," he says. "The fact that I'm an old farmer and work harder and faster than anyone else means I can do in a day what someone else would do in three. I also consider this to be creative work. I plant for color, texture, and height." Earl has no intention of relinquishing the job.

In a separate, walled-in garden just off the garden house, Earl raises vegetables. Ever mindful of his personal roots, he says, "It's very important to me to be able to raise and eat vegetables from my garden. Not having big bowls of tomatoes on the table in summer would feel wrong. This is one of the luxuries in life."

Another necessity for the ideal life-style, to Earl, is a home made entirely from old building materials scoured from all parts of the countryside. "We used nice old oak beams for the flooring, and in other sections, we used old pine boards," says Earl. In the foyer and living room, he transformed old pine boards into raised paneling.

The kitchen contains Mercer tiles—materials of special local historical interest. Henry Mercer operated a tile manufacturing business just four miles from the Jamison house from about 1910 to 1950. "I was lucky enough, when I bought a property, to come across a lot of these

Left *and* below: *A garden house was essential, given Earl's proclivity for turning the earth. Even here, a vintage look was achieved through weathered beams, pavers, and wood and antique red clay shingles. Plants provide an ever-changing landscape of color with the seasons: clematis vines drape the window, bleeding-heart infuses the verdant space with its brilliant hue, and climbing rose tops the doorway.*
Above: *The notion of a peaceable kingdom rings clearly from the gazebo, snuggled venerably into the grounds with its own attendant flowers.*

•••

P·E·A·C·E·A·B·L·E KINGDOM

Mercer tiles that had never been used," explains Earl. Unglazed Mercer tiles quickly were put to use as flooring in the kitchen, and glazed decorative tiles were inset in the deep windowsills.

True to its fabricated history, the home has a facade entirely of log and stone. "We used stones cleared off the property's hedgerows, and combined them for the right color combination with stones salvaged from an old barn," Earl says. Even the garden pavers are old.

The antiques that fill the Jamison home are no less a selective and deliberate part of Earl's plan. As the home itself is a testament to changes in time, Earl's collections reflect his changing interests—some passions, such as mechanical banks, ebbing with the years. Pottery, wood carvings, and certain primitives, however, have weathered the vicissitudes of time and tastes.

"I have always collected them. Tin horns I love because of their form and history. They were old barge or huckster horns and each has a different sound. I would never collect a brass horn because it wouldn't have the right feel or primitive quality," Earl explains.

And in his strangely but wonderfully venerable new home, getting it right is what it's all about. □

Below: *A majestic stone arch in the garden wall opens onto Earl's half-acre vegetable garden, which includes herbs to the left, vegetables in the center, and a few shrubs to the right, which are being propagated.*
Above: *An antique sheep weather vane guards a stone column at one end of the garden wall.*
Left: *Earl, Chee, and family.*

●●●

Triple Play

It's no easy feat moving three Vermont barns to Connecticut and blending them into a single, winning style. It puts the builder in a league by himself.

By Steve Cooper. Produced by Bonnie Maharam

Michael Greenberg is philosophical about building.

"Before the first nail is ever pounded in, I spend a great deal of time just thinking through how people will live in the house, how they will move around, every little detail.

"As a builder, I'm able to take a piece of land and create a sculpture where people will live. It's all very absorbing to me," says Michael, who earned a philosophy degree in college before launching into his hammers-and-nails career.

Best exemplifying the devotion to his craft is Michael's own house, which is actually three barns pegged together like a carpenter's version of a patchwork quilt. Humble shelters have been transformed into a playful, rambling amalgam of shapes and angles. It's a new math, where the sum

Above: *Although made from three separate barn structures, builder Michael Greenberg's Weston, Connecticut, home is unified by consistent exterior detailing.* Left: *Michael Greenberg.*

Triple Play

seems greater than its parts would suggest.

"I enjoy the old barn material. I love the feel, the character of it, the way it takes on such great color with age. It's different. It's nice and homey," he says.

Michael pulled his Vermont barns together 12 years ago. He first found a small granary, which became the kitchen. The second barn became the dining room and living room. The last created space for two bedrooms.

Erecting these aging structures again was no simple matter. Carefully disassembling barns at their site and rebuilding them at another is strenuous work. Old timbers may have rot, joints weaken, and handling every piece in

this elaborate puzzle is a struggle against crushing weights.

"I don't work with barns as often as I used to. They're so labor intensive. These aren't tract houses," Michael says.

He did, however, make an exception for his own

Right: *All of the timbers and siding seen in this dining room and loft area were once part of a Vermont barn. Michael built the fireplace using stone taken from the area surrounding his house.*
Top: *A 14-foot addition recently transformed this space from a small study into a living room.*
Above: *A dark English library table nicely complements the aged barn woods in the dining room.*

Triple Play

house recently. He added a master bedroom wing, expanded the kitchen, and more than doubled the living room's size.

"It was more than just wanting more space. I also wanted to improve the whole circulation of the house," Michael says. "When I started out, I had a rather small addition in mind, but then one thing led to another. It's actually become quite like the connected houses of old, where a homeowner would add a wing here and another there."

Chief among the benefits was a kitchen that grew from 300 to 450 square feet. Michael crafted strikingly beautiful and functional cabinets from aged-pine barn boards.

Michael says, "We fiddled around with some old wood and we actually ended up taking barn siding and hand planing the wood to skin off the very old look.

"We unified the boards by lightly pickling them (with a white stain) and then giving them ten coats of wax so they look like an old piece of furniture with a very nice hue."

The expansion also gave Michael a larger living room washed with light from a wall of windows.

"Mainly, the remodeling gave me more space. It also allowed me to use some newer, high-tech products that weren't available when I first built the house. The lighting, for instance: I was able to use pin lights and halogen lighting that weren't available. At night now, the place just glows," Michael says.

The expansion's most difficult aspect was

Right: *With glass on three sides and overhead, the kitchen eating area offers a sunny escape.*
Top: *Natural materials abound in a kitchen featuring Michael's handmade barn-board cabinets, 3-inch maple countertops, and work surface of Carrara marble. The floor is white oak planks.*
Above: *A small courtyard created during renovation was a perfect place for this cooking fireplace.*

Triple Play

tracking down a fresh supply of barn material. When he first began recycling structures in the mid-1970s, aging utility structures were plentifully scattered around New England. Now, however, they've become as rare as the family farm.

"There isn't the quantity of old barn materials around today that there was when I began. I still have my sources, but you have to look much harder to find good-quality materials," he says.

This lack of raw materials and the ever-shifting demands of the market have prodded Michael to build other types of houses.

"My style has evolved, reflecting different architectural times," he explains. "I have done everything from contemporary to shingle-style houses, which I am doing a little more of now. I am returning to a more rustic, smaller Connecticut type of architecture, where the spaces function well and are very livable."

So far he has constructed about 60 homes in Connecticut's richly wooded Fairfield County. Among his clients have been actor Robert

Redford and writer Erica Jong. Buyers are attracted by the region's tranquillity and access to New York City, he says.

"I cater to the upper end of the market. The area appeals to artistic, individualistic people, people who are attracted

by the uniqueness of the architecture and the site, people who are looking for something more than a typical four-bedroom."

These same qualities drew Michael. His barns nest in an environment that evokes a sense of permanence and harmony.

In turn, his house enhances the environment with its gracefully aged style. The ease of the architecture perfectly captures the mood of life in the woods.

"I'm still intrigued by the style of my house and it will always be my favorite kind of house," he says. "I never grow tired of living here. To me, it has always felt very rich and colorful and warm." □

Right: *The walls in the bedroom are old barn siding treated with only a wire brush and a vacuum.*
Top: *This crisp bathroom fits the house well with its nickel faucets and towel bars from Europe, black-and-white tiles, hand-painted sink, and marble countertop. Michael also built the vanity.*
Above: *This loft fireplace warms a cozy, secluded niche Michael favors for use as a study.*

Posey County
CONNOISSEUR

A native of southern Indiana and a longtime connoisseur of Posey County, Indiana, history, antiques, and artifacts, Jim Sanders might have seemed a likely candidate to restore one of the area's oldest homes. Indeed, in his job as executive director of Historic New Harmony, Indiana, he oversees the restoration of the town's historic section. But at home, he wanted the aura of authenticity without its inconveniences. "I did not want to live in a museum," Jim says.

Along with 20th-century comforts, Jim wanted a house with room to showcase his large collection of antiques, many of which were gleaned from area farms and homesteads. A collector since his teens, for years Jim had been stashing finds in buildings across the county. "I had to do something," he says jokingly. "There was not an empty storage space left."

To accommodate each special piece, Jim determined its placement before the layout of his house was finalized, then had the architect complete the plans according to those specifications. Doors were shifted to leave room for a dry sink or cabinet; windows moved to make way for a step-back cupboard or a highboy. Jim's penchant for southern hospitality also affected the house plans: He needed plenty of space for entertaining visitors— official and otherwise— who pass through town.

From the initial planning phase to finishing the wood

Above: *Jim Sanders, executive director of Historic New Harmony, is an expert on antiques and teaches many college-level classes on the subject. He is drawn to regional pieces and loves to share his favorites. Special items from his collection of Posey County antiques often find their way into New Harmony's historic buildings, where the visiting public can enjoy them.*
Left: *Jim Sanders built his 1840-style saltbox on an 8-acre tract bordering the Wabash River, a lush spot where the Harmonists once tended an orchard. An existing brick cottage, dating to the 1840s, was joined to the new house with a breezeway.*
Opposite: *The keeping room adjoining the kitchen exemplifies Jim Sanders' trademark style: fine country antiques displayed with a minimum of clutter. The maple trestle table at the keeping room's heart is from the 1880s.*

floors, Jim took a hands-on approach to his saltbox project, designating every detail of construction and interior design. He salvaged the wainscoting for the entryway from an 1820 Posey County house that was destined for the wrecking ball. Wild cherry from his family's farm in Posey County was used for bookshelves in the library. Most of the remaining woodwork was milled and crafted locally, as were the poplar floors—typical of the Harmonist era.

As planned, the house sets off Jim's collections in an eye-catching way. The rooms are uncluttered, with adequate space for viewing each piece, from a Posey County trestle table to a formal Tennessee hunt board.

Today, Jim's house, just two blocks from New Harmony's Main Street, seems right at home among its historic neighbors. With its classic saltbox lines, the simple structure could easily date from the 1840s, the time of New Harmony's afterglow period. Invited guests to Jim's home—of which there are many—are charmed by the resemblance to New Harmony's historic structures; casual passers-by are often confused. On the average of once a week the doorbell rings, and Jim opens the front door to find tourists hot on the history trail. A case of mistaken identity, perhaps, but a lucky one. Jim knows just where to send them. □

Opposite top: Though Jim favors Indiana furniture and artwork, he often buys antiques from adjacent states. Although more formal than the pieces in Jim's keeping room, the Tennessee-made hunt board and Kentucky-made corner cupboard here still display the simple forms typically used by country cabinetmakers. Presiding over all is a prim and proper portrait attributed to an Ohio artist.

Opposite, bottom left: Wood floors in the entryway and throughout the house are of native poplar, favored by the Harmonists because of the resistance to insect damage. Jim's pride in his Indiana roots is evident in his choice of wall covering: the formal-seeming wallpaper takes an agrarian turn in this reproduction pattern called Maize.

Opposite, bottom right: Pewter crafted by German immigrants to Indiana's Posey County fills a dining room cupboard.

Below: Simple lines are the common denominator shared by many of Jim's antiques, from a Sheraton highboy to a Chippendale secretary. Other elements, judiciously placed—bandboxes, quilts, coverlets, artwork—soften a potentially hard-edged look.

Because they share the same birthday, Jim has a special interest in President Ulysses S. Grant, a connection that has inspired a collection of Grant mementos, such as the portrait hanging here.

Linkin' Log HOME

Three historic log cabins connect into one wonderful Georgia home that's furnished in old Southern charm.

By Candace Ord Manroe
Produced by Ruth Reiter

Atlanta homes went up in clouds of thick black smoke as Sherman marched through the South, leaving behind little to gratify posterity's hankering for historic houses.

The impact of the general's campaign is still felt today, and not only by those who take an architectural approach to history. Some Atlanta antiques aficionados smart at a dilemma that's entirely their own—wonderful Southern collections, but scarcely a compatible place to put them.

Jim Lord, a new convert to country collectibles, was such a person. Eager to find a suitably seasoned home for what was fast becoming a commodious collection, he felt discouraged. It wasn't just Atlanta proper that had a paucity of historic houses, Jim discovered, but the entire metropolitan area.

Finding the right home was important. The chilly contemporary cluster house he shared with lifelong friend Bobby Dent, coworker in a computer firm, simply was not a consanguine spirit. And Jim was tired of warehousing his vintage finds in the garage.

Three historic log cabins were transplanted to the Atlanta area and joined to make one home.

Near right: *The living room's corner cupboard was the first major piece purchased by the homeowners. Next to it stands a beaded tapered-leg table with poplar top and yellow pine base from a Cherokee Indian home in northeast Georgia.*

Far right: *One of the home's best Southern antiques is a circa-1860 country Chippendale broken-pediment cupboard in the living room.*

Linkin' Log
HOME

"It took three years of looking before we found this house," Jim says.

This actually means three historic houses in one.

In a display of Southern ingenuity, three log cabins—one from Kentucky, two from Tennessee—had been dismantled and moved to the suburban Atlanta property, then connected by newly constructed dogtrots to form one home.

All the reassembly work to connect the cabins had been done by the previous owner, with only some fine-tuning and personal-preference changes required by the new buyers.

By virtue of number alone, the transplanted cabins more than compensated for Atlanta's deficiency of antebellum houses: Here was not only *one*, but *three* historic structures to call home.

And what was good for the homeowners also was good for the home. The dismantling and relocation of the cabins was, in fact, their elixir. The old buildings more than likely would have been demolished or ignored and allowed to disintegrate.

The three-in-one feature has another bonus: Each cabin brings its own unique history to the home.

Built around 1800, the cabin that composes the front of the home is a 1½-story structure originally located in Thomasville, Kentucky. In its new Georgia digs, it serves as the living room and the upstairs bedroom.

Also at the front of the home, and to the left of the central Kentucky structure, is a circa-1820 cabin that was moved from Carthage, Tennessee. This one-room cabin now serves as the downstairs bedroom.

The Tennessee cabin's original function, however, was as a country schoolhouse. It then was used as a church and, finally, as a modest home before becoming a pinion in today's larger three-in-one domicile.

Despite its minuscule size, the Tennessee cabin hosts a surprisingly assertive past: Resounding reminders of its history include the word "Christ"

Right: *Favorite collections of homeowner Jim Lord include antique children's shoes and, displayed Shaker-style from pegboard, children's chairs still bearing their original paint.*

Above: *The focal point of the living room is a flagstone fireplace with a wormy chestnut-log mantel. The worktable turned cocktail table was purchased for its original paint, as was the secretary.*

Above: *A collection of Southern pottery including pitchers, jugs, face jugs, and forms is displayed in the dining room window. The pieces work well with an old farm table in its original paint and a stepback cupboard from Dooley County, Georgia, that still boasts its original red color. The light fixture is a reproduction.*

Right: *A reproduction Noah's ark by Charlie Royston, of Atlanta, rests on a hunt board.*

Linkin' Log HOME

carved into one of the interior logs, from the cabin's early days as a church house.

The third cabin constitutes the back of the home—the kitchen and keeping room. Built in 1830, it was moved to Georgia from Smithville, Tennessee. It, too, is a testament to the past.

"When that cabin was built, it was a common practice of the day to line the logs with newspaper," says Bobby. The Smithville cabin was no exception. One newspaper liner of particular interest—and which, thankfully, was left intact during a recent cleaning of the logs and chinking—is an article on Andrew Jackson.

Even though the three cabin components of the house aren't indigenous to Georgia, their roots are purely Southern. That, and the warm country character of the rustic logs, make the home an ideal showcase for robust Southern antiques.

"When I first started collecting these pieces, my roommate thought I had lost my mind," recalls Jim. "We lived in an ultra-contemporary home, and I was bringing in things that he thought were firewood."

Eventually, though, the country collectibles proved too inviting. Bobby's anti-antiques foothold, and with it, his bias favoring contemporary design, was slipping. Soon he was a country devotee in his own right, planting a purchase solidly amid those furnishings and accessories that smack of the past and of the primitive.

"He fell in love with Southern country antiques, and his passion for collecting matched my own," says Jim.

Getting to that point took some time, however. "I'm the kind of person who doesn't like a lot of change," says Bobby. "I was accustomed to a stark, contemporary home. But after a while, I started appreciating country. Although I'm now developing a taste for more formal country, I appreciate it all. There will always be a place in my life for country."

Bobby's particular penchants extend to graniteware and country

Right: *The homeowners spend most of their time in the keeping room, which combines the kitchen work area with comfortable seating space. Filled with blue-and-white enamelware, the room is dominated by chairs (in their original blue paint) from Laurens County, Georgia, and an old two-board top table with tapered legs. Between two upholstered chairs stands a Virginia chest decorated in its original sponge paint.*

Above: *The downstairs bedroom, just off a short hallway from the living room, features the same unfinished pine flooring found throughout the home—but is topped with an Amish rug. As elsewhere, reproductions meld with antiques: The bed is a reproduction Georgia piece, while the footboard's yellow pine chest from Habersham County, Georgia, dates to 1850* or 1860. A mustard secretary is from Newton County, Georgia, circa 1870, and was purchased from a physician's office. The rocking horse is Jim's favorite. Right: Jim's mother quilted the bedroom's stellar schoolhouse quilt as a housewarming gift. An early find was the red chest of drawers from Houston County, Georgia; it is made of walnut, with yellow pine as a secondary wood.

74

Linkin' Log HOME

textiles—he's responsible for most of the calicoes in the home.

Jim, in contrast, thrives on change. Once he made the leap from contemporary to country, he couldn't collect quickly enough, or with enough range of diversity.

"I would have to classify myself as a compulsive collector," he admits.

Proof is his collection of children's chairs, many of which hang, Shaker-style, from pegboard on the wall. "I love children's chairs," Jim begins. "It was amazing to me that here was something very, very affordable, and with its original paint."

Instead of gradually assembling a collection, Jim "bought twenty or twenty-five children's chairs in a short time, then saw something else I liked and pursued that," he says.

"I like all of the antiques in the home an awful lot, but none I've bought are life or limb to me. Furniture is not to die for—it's a material possession. It's exciting to find something new and different, and to change pieces," Jim adds.

He is not totally fickle, however. A

few collections such as blue-and-white enamelware and children's shoes have enjoyed a greater longevity with him. "These I find continually intriguing," he says.

Regardless of what's next on the horizon in Jim's ever-changing landscape of collectibles, there is one constant: "My real love is for the impractical. Rocking horses, wagons, antiques that are absolutely useless," he says.

This really is more than just a predilection: It's a philosophy. "You can fill up a room with fine furniture, but it's the accessories that make it interesting and that make it home," says Jim. "Entering a home that's decorated in this manner is certainly not like going to a department store."

To facilitate his goal of frequently switching or augmenting collections, Jim started his own antiques business while continuing his career in the computer industry. "The plan was to just become involved with antiques shows so that I could be aware of what was going on, and to make enough money to be able to buy a piece now and then," he says.

Right: With half-timbered, under-the-eaves walls and collections of children's chairs and clothing, the upstairs bedroom is especially cozy. A reproduction rope bed is an exact copy of a Georgia antique. Dressing it is a red star quilt from Kentucky that is signed and dated 1880. Old rag rugs—flea market finds—were stitched together to form the floor covering.

Linkin' Log HOME

Above: *Jim Lord (seated) and Bobby Dent are lifelong friends, having grown up in small Georgia towns 20 miles apart where one's father was a country preacher, the other's, a car dealer.* Below: *Spacious porches grace the cabin.*

His sharp eye for quality, and his specialization in Southern furniture, however, have garnered considerable reputation and respect for Jim among serious collectors and dealers.

For their home, Jim and Bobby buy from houses and dealers. Their furniture is Southern, but many accessories are from Ohio and Pennsylvania.

Typically, they buy furniture in the rough—pieces that require cleaning and restoring. "There's no crime in saving furniture," says Bobby.

Nor do they find it objectionable to intersperse a few reproductions with antiques. "I wish everything was old," reasons Jim, "but I don't have unlimited money. Can I really afford to pay two thousand dollars for an old sampler, or am I happy with the look, for thirty-five dollars?"

After a cluster contemporary home and now this current cluster of log cabins, what next?

"It's off to the Texas Hill Country to open an antiques shop and become innkeepers at the Comfort Common, a limestone B&B in Comfort," says Jim.

As for the style of the historic inn, he confirms: "Pure country." □

June

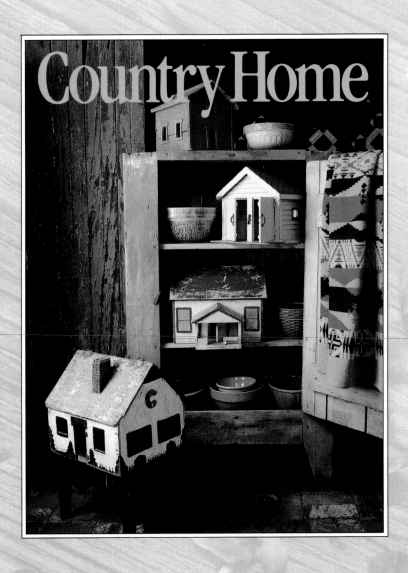

LIVING
WITH THE
LEGACY

Steve Bengel's Craftsman-style retreat in Eureka Springs, Arkansas, is an Arts and Crafts experience—outfitted with furniture from the movement's heyday.

By Candace Ord Manroe. Produced by Mary Anne Thomson

Above: *Steve Bengel appreciates the Arts and Crafts style of his circa-1906 home.* Opposite: *Dining chairs are transitional with features of both Art Nouveau and Arts and Crafts style.*

☐ ☐ ☐

In the Ozark Mountains outside Eureka Springs, life kicks back—a generation or two—for Memphis, Tennessee, designer Steve Bengel. Steve's Arkansas vacation home is his retreat not only from day-to-day demands, but from time itself.

"Friends who visited said they didn't think they could ever go back to their grandmother's house, but that when they got here, they had a sense of having gone home again," observes Steve.

"There's just a wonderful aura about the place," he says.

The sensation is more than ordinary time warp. It is a special nostalgia issuing from a blend of simplicity and quality, which can be ascribed to the home's Arts and Crafts architecture and furnishings.

Built in 1906, the home possibly was constructed from one of the authentic Craftsman designs of Gustav Stickley, turn-of-the-century America's best-known Arts and Crafts designer. Whether the home was built on speculation from a pattern book or as a custom design is not known.

What is evident, however, is the structure's careful attention to detail and its no-frills sensibility—characteristics that show the influence of America's Arts and Crafts Movement at the turn of the century.

Typical of an Arts and Crafts building, the home was constructed using indigenous materials: local onyx on the fireplace, red and white oak on the woodwork, floors, and beams. Its linear geometrics, especially on the ceiling, are another hallmark of Arts and Crafts design, as are the home's hand-hammered copper fixtures.

The strong but clean architecture demanded like furniture.

"Everything is pretty much of the Arts and Crafts period, and most of the pieces I found in the area," says Steve.

Photographs: William N. Hopkins, Hopkins Associates.

LIVING
WITH THE
LEGACY

No matter that mission oak (best-known of Arts and Crafts furnishings) is not the style to which Steve ordinarily would gravitate.

"The style of furnishings I live with in Memphis couldn't be more different," he says. "There, I have needlepoint tapestries and mahogany

□ □ □

Above: *The hearth is made of onyx gathered from a cave only 10 miles away.*
Right: *Ozarks-crafted baskets top an antique cupboard with hand-blown glass in the kitchen.*
Opposite: *White and red oak in the living room are indigenous to the area.*

furniture—a more formal feeling."

The Arts and Crafts pieces in his Eureka Springs home, on the other

hand, "are straighter and cleaner. And the home itself is lighter, not overaccessorized. This is all in keeping with the way I believe a vacation home should be," says Steve.

Arts and Crafts furniture and architecture also are low-maintenance—sturdily constructed for longevity, with minimal repairs—another reason Steve finds them especially compatible with a vacation home.

Steve first remembers seeing the house as a 10-year-old child visiting the area on family vacation.

"We were leaf peepers. I had cousins who went to school there, and every fall we'd come up for a football game. In 1963, I wrote my grandparents that I had found the neatest place in the world and that, someday, I would live

magnolia and cedar—that convinced him to make an offer when the property was for sale 10 years ago.

"Certainly it wasn't the interior that attracted me. Everything had been done in New England colonial, and it was all wrong in this house. The two periods shouldn't have been mixed," insists Steve.

Once he remedied that, Steve was free to pursue what he loves best: using the home as a comfortable base for backpacking, canoeing, and hiking. He explains, "I don't consider this place a storehouse for treasures. It's for memories and experiences."

Arts and Crafts designers like Gustav Stickley and Frank Lloyd Wright would approve. □

there. I was twelve years old at the time," says Steve. As a child, he didn't yet have an appreciation for Arts and Crafts architecture. "It was the land I loved," he says.

And it was the land—4½ acres blanketed in red dogwoods, maples, oaks, sycamores, and even bay

□ □ □

Above: *A hand-hammered copper plate adds Arts and Crafts flavor to the solid oak hand-pegged trestle table.*
Right: *Family pieces—hatboxes, fan, chair—fill the bedroom, which also displays Steve's textiles collection.*

Cabin Comfort

In Bartlesville, Oklahoma, Jane and Jim Webb cache company away in a historic log cabin behind their New England-style saltbox home.

Produced by Nancy E. Ingram

At the turn of the century, a family of 10 occupied Jane and Jim Webb's Civil War-era guest cabin, holding square dances in the humble dwelling every Saturday night. A chicken thief, turned fugitive from justice, once holed up there. And in 1939, MGM's *Jesse James,* starring Tyrone Power, Henry Fonda, and Randolph Scott, opened with film footage of the cabin.

These are tamer days, though, and the old chink-and-daub log home isn't quite the host it once was to the wilder side of life.

Instead, it is host, in serene and gracious fashion, to the Webbs' house guests, having been moved—one slow log at a time—in 1983 from Pineville, Missouri, to the couple's residence in Bartlesville, Oklahoma.

Getting the siting just right was a major consideration. Jane and Jim wanted to be sure that visiting friends and relatives would be able to enjoy an enviable ambience, as well as complete privacy.

Ensconced in woods reminiscent of pioneer days, just beyond a hillside covered with dogwoods,

Above: *Almost as much as the fortunate friends who get to stay there, Jane and Jim Webb love the restored Civil War-era log cabin that they moved onto their property to use as a guesthouse for overnight visitors.*
Opposite: *The Webbs painstakingly moved the cabin from its original Pineville, Missouri, location to its new home in Oklahoma.*

Cabin Comfort

daffodils, ferns, and wildflowers, the two-story cabin is separated from the Webbs' New England-style saltbox home by a formal garden.

In addition to providing a pleasing view, the arduous efforts of Jane and Jim also give guests a realistic glimpse at early American country life.

The cabin is a true restoration, not a redo, with many of the original features intact. It features hand-hewn square logs, old window glass—half of which was original to the home—and wood floors that were discovered buried beneath mounds of old newspapers and linoleum.

Beyond all of this, the Webbs furnished the cabin completely in 18th- and 19th-century antiques collected from New England to Mississippi, where they both grew up.

Except for outfitting the cabin with electricity and central heating and air, the Webbs took great pains to make sure the old building was as authentic to the era as possible.

Unable to find appropriate antique light fixtures, Jane, for example, wasn't satisfied merely to furnish the guesthouse with reproduction tin sconces.

"They looked too new when we got them, so I buried them in the dirt and then watered them every day until they looked really rusty and more authentic," she explains. "Then I oiled them with dirty crankcase oil."

For the friends who stay there, the cabin represents a true labor of love. Unusual in this age of specialization, Jane and Jim didn't rely on anyone's muscle but their own and son Jimmy's to dismantle and ready the cabin.

Every weekend for three months, they drove the 100 miles from their home to the cabin's location in Missouri, where they would engage in such pastimes as hand-scrubbing the interior logs to rid them of yellow paint that had been added sometime after the cabin was built.

Their hands-on approach had its rewards. When the couple disassembled the cabin, they were pleased to discover the daubing consisted of such colorful materials as horsehair, rags, and paper.

Once they had liberated all of the logs from their chinking, the Webbs painstakingly identified each one with metal tags to assure that the cabin would be correctly rebuilt after the move.

Come reassembly time back in Oklahoma, Jim and Jane were just as determined to do things the hard—and right—way. They used no mechanical

Opposite: The Webbs hauled stones from a nearby pasture, then built the large cooking fireplace themselves where the original once stood. Each stone had to fit like a puzzle, which meant much discarding and tedious work. Although the fireplace appears to be true dry-stacked stone, for permanence, mortar is hidden deep between the stones.
Above: An 1800s cupboard holds quilts that Jane and Jim have collected.

means to hoist and stack the logs but relied, instead, on the old-fashioned method of pulling the logs in place with ropes—the same means that would have been used when the cabin originally was built.

Wanting their guests to be as comfortable as possible, Jane and Jim did make a few concessions to modernity. They placed fiberglass insulation between the logs and trowled over it with daubing.

And in true do-it-yourself fashion, Jane did all of the daubing.

The few elements of the cabin that are not original include the roof and the sill log. But here, too, the Webbs refused to settle for anything less than period authenticity, using materials old in style, if not in age.

The original wood shingles had long been covered with roll roofing and then corrugated tin, and the Webbs determined

Left: *Cat "Punkin" is cozy on a feather mattress topped with a rare log-cabin quilt in the cabin's sleeping area.*
Above: *An early rope bed with original red paint and tightening key at foot is to the left of the front door. The bed is dressed in a Solomon's crown quilt. A sampler dated 1790 hangs above the headboard, and an antique overshot weave coverlet drapes over the split-bark seat rocker.*
Right: *Herbs from the garden dry on beams.*

it was time for a return to bygone—in this case, better—days. They replaced the roof with wood shingles just like the originals. Each shingle was hand-split by a 75-year-old Arkansas man, who also split all the rails for the cabin's fencing.

To replace the rotten sill log, Jane and Jim actually purchased a second, smaller log cabin to use as "parts." Not only did they obtain a historic sill log in the process, but also enough extra logs to accommodate construction of a full bath attached to the back of the cabin, as well as an additional lean-to to hide the central heat and air equipment.

The purist approach—long hours, muscle aches, and all—has its payoffs. Last summer, friends took their wedding vows outside the cabin, beneath the wisteria arbor, and spent the first two nights of

married life in the cabin before leaving on their honeymoon.

The Webbs' physical, financial, and emotional investment in the cabin doesn't require any romantic rewards, however. It is reward in itself. Jane explains it simply: "We love a project." □

Beach House

ON THE PRAIRIE

A California-style carriage house on an Omaha horse farm is a delightful departure from the prairie for Jan and Mick Moriarty's lucky guests.

Produced by Candace Ord Manroe

On the fringe of the Nebraska prairie just outside Omaha, the white-on-white carriage house of Mick and Jan Mactier Moriarty represents a clean break from the predictable.

More beach house than farmhouse, the building is a paean to the pleasures of California living. From its bleached floors and all-white ceiling boards and exposed beams, to its pale, overscaled chairs and sofa, the carriage house belies its Midwestern geography in sunny, seashore style.

"I spent a lot of summers at Southampton and on the coast of Maine and have always loved the beach. When I saw a picture of a Malibu beach house in a magazine, I knew that was what I wanted here," says Jan.

Built in time for Jan and Mick's woodland wedding on the 300-acre property four years ago, the carriage house was a convenient dressing area for members of the wedding party. Then, when the newlyweds were remodeling the main house—an 1867 farmhouse just across the drive—the

Right: *Mick and Jan Moriarty treat their son Mac to a ride by the carriage house.*
Left *and* above: *A central room accommodates guests, serving as sleeping, living, and dining area. A screened-in sleeping porch adjoins the room.*

carriage house served as home.

These days, it's where friends or business associates visiting the

Photographs: WM Hopkins, Hopkins Associates. Design consultant: Allen Coleman, Allen Furniture.

family's horse-breeding farm and sports-horse complex, Ponca Farm, stay overnight.

From the exterior, the carriage house blends harmoniously into its environs. Just across the drive from the main house, it is clad in the same white clapboard as the farmhouse. Its gambrel roofline, too, is in the tradition of the region's vernacular architecture, particularly for barns.

But inside, the guesthouse forgets its roots. The expected dark woods simply are not to be found, replaced by a whitewashed palette that suggests a gentle bleaching in the sun.

"For furniture, we went with the soft comfort and oversize proportions associated with California style," says design consultant Allen Coleman. Natural, muted fabrics were chosen for upholsteries, reinforcing the clean and subtle contemporary look.

But the carriage house is not purely contemporary. To its modern nuances, Jan has brought country warmth. Her years of collecting American antiques and handcrafted oddities infuse the design with one-of-a-kind personality and, also, with sparkling color.

"She had a chicken coop full of antiques," says Allen, "and I helped her determine which of those would best work with the design. She really just needed somebody to give her a nudge. I gave advice

and, at times, surprised her. The project just flowed. We were like two kids playing," he says.

Most of the antiques are from Pennsylvania, where Jan lived while showing horses, or from Omaha, from which she is a native.

"The influence of both my grandmothers shadows my life greatly, including what and why I collect. Grandma Mac, my father's mother, was a mad collector of everything. Her home was fascinating.

"I like the eclectic—primitive or handcrafted pieces that are unique or odd," Jan explains.

With those in place, "all that's missing now," she adds, "is the ocean."

Left: *An antique garden gate and hooked rugs add warmth to the main room.*
Above: *Old animal cutouts decorate the quarters below.*

Little Caboose
T H A T   C O U L D

Company feels downright regal in Ann and Bob Kerr's caboose-turned-guesthouse in Ardmore, Oklahoma.

Produced by Nancy E. Ingram

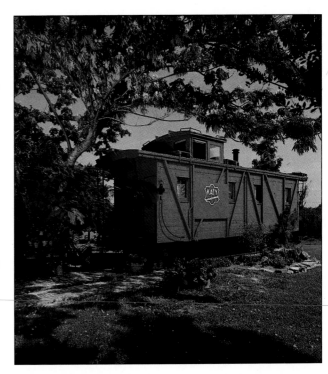

I n railroad jargon, they were known as "crummies"—the tail end of the train where railmen worked, ate, slept, and stayed protected from summer heat and winter cold.

When Bob and Ann Kerr found their own crummy, Katy Caboose #33, the name fit. The caboose had been abandoned for 12 years in a field outside of town. Its most recent inhabitants were varmints, not trainmen.

Fortunately, the Kerrs had vision. They knew that, given benefit of their hard work and imagination, the caboose could provide not only shelter but a novel overnight experience as a guesthouse to visiting friends.

But translating vision into reality required patience. "We had to wait almost a year for the ground to be dry enough to move the caboose the three

or four miles over pasture and the fifteen miles to our backyard," says Ann.

Moving the caboose demanded a 100-ton oil-field crane and two 14-wheel flatbed trucks—one truck for the caboose and another for the wheels.

In the spirit of an old-fashioned barn raising, friends and family turned out for a "track-laying"—laying 20 feet of railroad track on a gravel bed as a fitting foundation for the caboose in its new location.

And then the real work began. The Kerrs completely gutted the caboose, leaving only the cupola and the original metal stairs.

Below: *Bob and Ann Kerr admire the view from the crow's nest of their 1920s caboose above.*
Left: *The sitting room emulates a parlor car.*

Photographs: Gene Johnson.

immediately put to use, paid off.

"You would be amazed at what we were able to incorporate into the caboose that was bought for no particular purpose at the time," says Bob.

Pillars that had been deemed a "find," then stashed in the barn for years, were resurrected and notched to fit in the wall between the bunk beds and parlor.

"They disguise an area that was sort of nondescript and give the impression of another window," explains Bob.

For the comfort of their guests, the couple equipped the kitchen area with a sink and small refrigerator. A built-in coffeemaker and toaster-oven suffice for cooking needs. A heat pump cools and heats the caboose, which still features its original sink in the bathroom.

These days, there's nothing bare bones about the old railcar. More than a rustic refuge from the elements, it is beneficiary to the Kerrs' special decorative flair.

"We wanted the caboose to look like what we imagined the old private parlor cars of the rail barons might have looked like," says Ann.

"We interpreted that to mean including elements such as paneling, rich upholstery, mementos. Some of the special things we simply brought out from the house. Junkers always have too much stuff anyway," she says. □

Above: *Bunk beds were built under the cupola, each outfitted with large underneath storage drawers as well as a small hanging closet tucked under each side of the crow's nest. Colorful woven textiles add warmth.*

For a period feeling, they installed a tin ceiling salvaged from a turn-of-the-century building. To inject a more formal flavor, they covered the rough walls in fabric. Although the caboose's original hardware was utilized, its 16 windows had to be replaced.

"Bob and our sons, Dick and Karl, did all the work except for the actual carpentry. Another friend who is a master cabinetmaker did that," says Ann.

Years of scouring flea markets and tag sales, stocking interesting collectibles they couldn't

COTTAGE COMEBACK

*When vacation fever strikes, this **Country Home**® magazine renovation on the Potomac River should be the cure. The transformation of this forlorn, early-1950s retreat is just what the doctor ordered.*

By Steve Cooper
Produced by
Eileen A. Deymier

Photographs: Tim Fields.
Siding, CertainTeed Corp.; windows and door, Eagle Window and Door; fabrics, Brunschwig & Fils

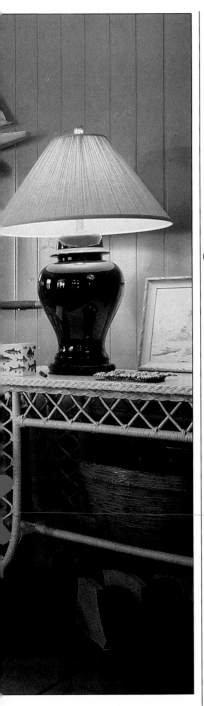

COTTAGE COMEBACK

Block walls can be cold and hostile. When simply stacked in rudimentary style with little architectural imagination, they are a damp, dank, and joyless gray barrier. Lacking subtlety, they won't bend or give or make room for expansion.

Such was this 1950s Virginia cottage. A cast-off castaway. A getaway that got away.

Though perched at water's edge where the Potomac River flows into picturesque Chesapeake Bay, this basic brick box wasn't part of the setting's natural romantic ambience. It was Cinderella after the stroke of midnight. Drab, down-at-the-mouth, and searching for a wand.

Then, magic stirred as *Country Home*® magazine editors joined with Baltimore designer Stephen O'Brien of The H. Chambers Co. to infuse the doleful domicile with new vitality as a vacation home. This kind of design sorcery could transform any common dwelling into royalty. Of course, it takes more than the wave of a conjurer's magic scepter. It's the result of design vision, careful selection of building materials, and skill.

The result is a friendly, comfy two-bedroom home well suited for four visitors—six in a pinch—any time of year. It's still a study in simplicity. But that doesn't mean it has to be drafty, gloomy, or cheerless.

"We designed it as a weekend getaway for urban dwellers in search of a carefree refuge from their frantic everyday lives," says project coordinator Eileen Deymier, *Country Home* magazine regional editor in Baltimore.

The house is located in an area of marshes, creeks, and inlets where Virginia's Northern Neck juts into the river. The Neck, as it is called by locals, is an area rich in historic sites. At the upper end are George Washington's birthplace and the ancestral home of the Lee family. At the lower end there are colonial churches, plantations, and villages dating back 200 years. Because peace and quiet are the region's most precious assets, it's gaining popularity as a weekend retreat for the harried residents of Washington,

Far left: *New fiberglass roof shingles, insulating windows, and vinyl siding lift the face of the river cottage. This view looks toward the sun porch from near water's edge.*
Left: *A "before" shot of the living area.*

❑ ❑ ❑

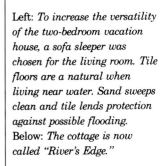

Left: *To increase the versatility of the two-bedroom vacation house, a sofa sleeper was chosen for the living room. Tile floors are a natural when living near water. Sand sweeps clean and tile lends protection against possible flooding.*
Below: *The cottage is now called "River's Edge."*

❑ ❑ ❑

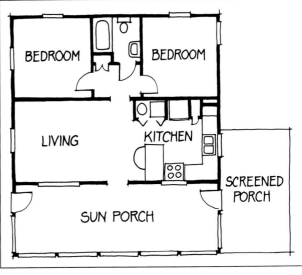

Above: Skylight, Velux-America, Inc.; roofing, Owens-Corning Fiberglas Corp.; siding, CertainTeed Corp. Illustration: Carson Ode

COTTAGE COMEBACK

Far left: *From left to right, builder Hiram H. King Jr.; his son and assistant, Donald King; designer Stephen O'Brien; and project coordinator Eileen Deymier.*
Left: *The sun-room during renovation.*

□ □ □

D.C., which is about a two-hour drive to the north.

Though the riverside cottage was not renovated to become a full-time residence, builders couldn't skimp on quality. Harsh winter storms pounding the coastline here would quickly ferret out any material weakness.

Like most renovation projects, work began with the dismantler's crowbar. The house was picked as cleanly as the local catch when it's ready for a frying pan. Long banks of jalousie windows were removed, wall paneling ripped out, kitchen cabinets torn away, doors taken off their hinges, the roof pried up, and the bathroom emptied of well-worn fixtures.

When the stripping process was complete, the house was little more than a 30-foot, cinder-block square with rooms arranged into narrow corridors. It was ready for a thorough rebuilding.

The goal was to transform an otherwise unremarkable house into one with style and character. As with any renovation project, this had to be accomplished within the limitations presented by the preexisting shell. This wasn't a blank architectural slate, but rather a basic structure where redesign of rooms, windows, and doors would be restricted by original block walls.

Several significant changes help bring a fresh, comfortable redefinition to the house. These start with an expanded sun-room running the length of the northeastern side. The view has been opened with a bank of 14 energy-efficient, double-hung windows facing the river.

Before renovation, this space was an add-on with an enclosed porch and a poorly placed makeshift bedroom. The windows were jalousies—louvered windows that open by cranking, break up scenic views with horizontal lines, and leak terribly during storms. Situated in the middle of this wall of windows was a single entry door. Stylistically, the

Left: *Nine wicker pieces for this sun porch and the living room were found after numerous trips to auctions, thrift shops, and estate sales. Because each is painted white and the same fabrics are used throughout, furniture is easily grouped and regrouped into any combination of settings.*
Below: *This room faces northeast, and during storms it gets hammered. So extra-efficient insulating windows were installed. They are as tall as would fit—giving the room a feeling of added height.*

□ □ □

Above and top left: Windows and door, Eagle Window and Door; tile, Summitville Tiles; ceiling and wall paneling, Georgia-Pacific Corp.; ceiling fan, Hunter Fan; yellow fabric and floral chintz, Brunschwig & Fils; hot-pink trim and table skirt fabric, Stroheim & Romann, Inc.

101

porch was equivalent to wearing brown oxfords with a colorful sunsuit.

As a key element in the make-over, the new windows are designed with gas-filled, dual-sealed glass for maximum insulation, about twice the effectiveness of typical insulated glass. What this means to consumers became apparent during a recent storm. While a fierce, howling wind of about 60 miles per hour and raged against the cottage, O'Brien says rooms were so "absolutely tight, you could barely even hear the wind."

At each end of the sun-room, entry doors were added by veteran builder Hiram King Jr. French doors with full glass were chosen for the extra sunlight and expanded view they offer.

For exterior durability, a new roof was applied. The heavyweight, fiberglass roofing shingles have the look of shakes and a 40-year warranty.

A newly introduced line of vinyl siding and trim was chosen because it reproduces the appearance of early 20th-century wood without the maintenance concerns. The manufacturer offers a style guide and system demonstration kit to assist in choosing colors and trim. These include trim samples allowing customers to determine how different types suit their home.

O'Brien chose wide trim around doors and windows to give vertical emphasis to the low-slung house.

"We did not want to use shutters because they emphasize the horizontal. So the moldings really became critical to the overall look of the finished project. These new trim options, the three-and-a-half-inch-wide lineals, emphasized the vertical, which improves the exterior tremendously," he says.

After settling on the exterior materials, O'Brien wanted to achieve a welcoming, cottage feel throughout the interior. A key to this was installation of brightly painted, grooved wooden paneling throughout the interior and pale blue bead board for ceilings. Panels mask lifeless block walls yet lend an air of take-your-shoes-off hominess. Paneling also allowed the installation of an additional layer of insulation on walls.

Though the living room and sun-room are closely

Above: Semicircular kitchen snack table has a tile surface matching other countertops. The kitchen was designed by Alan Caplan/Stuart Kitchens in Baltimore.

Below: *An English-style plate rack makes organizing a snap even for first-time visitors. Tiles graced with vegetable designs are just right for the kitchen. Renovating is a messy job, as attested to by the bottom picture.*

☐ ☐ ☐

COTTAGE COMEBACK

related, they were treated as separate spaces before the renovation. O'Brien tied them together visually with paneling, tile floor throughout, similar wicker furnishings, vibrant fabrics, and the removal of a door that once divided the rooms. A pair of windows in the block wall between the two rooms was also removed to afford unobstructed views of the river.

Ultimately, the cottage's atmosphere depends on color. O'Brien wasn't shy about hot pinks or zesty yellows.

"You can afford to be bold with color in a weekend house.... Many would not have chosen a pumpkin color for the living room, erroneously thinking that beige or white might make it appear larger. The fact is this room will never feel like a big room. By using a strong, warm color, we enhanced the feeling of coziness," O'Brien says.

The kitchen was given its own coziness when an exterior door was walled up. This rerouted traffic so visitors wouldn't enter through the kitchen, and it allowed for an efficient, U-shape mealtime work area designed by Alan Caplan, CKD/Stuart Kitchens in Baltimore. Stripping away old kitchen wall paneling also revealed an original window. It was removed and the space became a convenient pass-through from the kitchen to the sun-room.

In the bathroom, a fresh batch of fixtures was installed and a skylight was added to bathe the room in a steady stream of sunshine. The room was finished with a handsome curved vanity from Pennsylvania cabinetmaker Kevin Dagliano and a whimsical trompe l'oeil window, which was created by artist Wayne Hand, of Baltimore.

Throughout the home, a theme of visual richness is maintained. So the Potomac River cottage has come back, indeed. Even a block house from 1953 can be refreshed and renewed given a large dose of skillful care. □

Right: This cramped, 10-foot-square bedroom gets an element of visual surprise with a cheerfully painted yellow school desk, a brilliantly colored comforter, and abundant, floral chintz window treatments.
Below: Designer O'Brien emphasized the stripe on the balloon curtains by using lined sheets, a narrow-stripe dust skirt, and plaid blankets.
Left: Keeping conservation in mind, the toilet needs only 1.4 gallons per flush. Artist Wayne Hand's work masquerades as a window, and a skylight provides natural light.

□ □ □

Above, right: Plaid blanket, Ralph Lauren Home Collection; ceiling and wall paneling, Georgia-Pacific Corp.
Above, left: Tub, sink, toilet, Eljer Industries; skylight, Velux-America; tiles, Summitville Tiles. Opposite: Fan, Hunter Fan; sheets, Wamsutta; floral fabric, Brunschwig & Fils

August

SECONDHAND
Sanctuary

*René Parker salvages
a place of her own.*

By Steve Cooper   Produced with Bonnie Warren

Photographs: William N. Hopkins, Hopkins Associates. Gardens: David Richmond

107

On the day René Parker enters Heaven's portals, her friends are certain she'll cast etiquette aside and cheerfully offer gatekeepers some styling advice. It won't be from conceit, but from a desire to share her personal design vision.

"My friends joke and say, 'Oh, René, He's [God] not ready for you.' They can see me walking up to the pearly gates, stopping, and saying, 'How about some old shutters over here and maybe some French doors retrieved from a salvage yard? And how are the gardens here?'" says René, with a ready laugh.

With a strong style sense developed during extensive travels throughout North America and Europe, René has spent the last six years orchestrating the metamorphosis of her ordinary, suburban New Orleans ranch house into an earthy, romantic cottage. A sumptuous garden and innovative use of recycled doors, windows, and other building elements are the hallmarks of her magician's touch.

The results perfectly mirror René herself. The home is lighthearted, breezy, feminine, and very down-to-earth. Goldilocks would pronounce this cottage "just right."

"I set out to create my own little bit of heaven on earth, you might say, and enjoy it. It's my sanctuary," says René, a

Delta Air Lines flight attendant for 23 years.

She gathered ideas during stays in England, Ireland, and France. A lengthy sojourn in Switzerland was a primary source of inspiration.

From the Swiss, René came away with the understanding that doors and windows aren't simply utilitarian devices, but part of the design scheme. She also discovered the beauty of bare wood.

Various influences converged into a single concept the first time she watched the movie *On Golden Pond.*

"When I saw that movie, with all those old, squeaking doors, I knew that was what I wanted. I wanted that sound. It conveys a feeling of something that has stood the test of time," she says.

It wasn't long before René donned work clothes and started frequenting a New Orleans secondhand building-materials dealer, Carrollton Lumber and Wrecking. Picking a careful path through the salvage yard, she found bargain windows, doors, and plumbing.

"Those who love flea markets will find a salvage yard is much like that. A kind of wonderful, outdoor, help-thyself place where you can find five- and ten-dollar doors," she says.

When she gets her treasures home, she does much of the work herself. Major installations are handled by general contractor Larry Roussell. Though she says it hasn't always been easy for him, he invariably finds a way to accommodate René's ever-evolving brainstorms. The two have struck a deal: She pays, he does the work. No questions.

"This is where being an independent woman is so

Sanctuary

wonderful. There's no husband to challenge me and say, 'Why would we do that, René?' I have a good vision of what I want to achieve," she says.

The make-over didn't actually begin in the house, but with the garden. As always, she has her own way of looking at outdoor design—calling the garden her favorite room. It reminds her of the greenery she enjoyed as a girl at her great-grandmother's house.

An oasis of green growth, René's backyard is alive with periwinkles, impatiens, salvias, and flowering purples and pinks. The garden is a free-form tangle where a brick walkway winds a stealthy path among the greenery.

With the benefit of Louisiana's 10-month growing season, René is able to keep the boundary between house and garden intentionally vague. The addition of a sun porch, larger windows, and glazed doors blurs the line between interior and exterior by making her garden a visual element of her interior style. Inside the house, flora continues with abundant dried flowers and potted plants.

Here's a room-by-room glimpse of her ideas:

Living room. Her least-used room, this is more of a gallery for objects, including some of her great-grandmother's crochet work.

A long, narrow room, the view is left airy by entry through two pairs of glazed French doors,

Left: *Old, arching shutters lend an earthy touch.*
Above: *René's love for baskets spans the globe. Their muted, natural colors appeal to her.*
"I'll go into a fruit or vegetable market in a country where they speak little English and somehow get them to realize I want to buy their baskets, not what's in them."
Below: *The back deck.*

Sanctuary

which—no surprise here—are salvaged.

René replaced the tract-house front window with a visually intricate, arching window. She also removed rooms of wall-to-wall carpet. The living room now has a floor of oak squares given a pickled look by a water-thin whitewashing tinted with a touch of pink.

Sun porch. When she bought the home, direct exit to the backyard was through a sliding glass door. The sun-room grew through a series of building steps. It began as a simple bark-covered patio and was finally enclosed with recycled windows.

"It's my little French café now and the place where friends usually sit when I have guests at the house," she says.

Kitchen. René gave cabinets her own touch by replacing doors. She gave each a simple picture-frame door with a wire-mesh screen insert painted white. While allowing some view into cabinet space, it doesn't make dishes a focal point.

A few modern machines had to go. She pulled out a dishwasher and the garbage disposal.

"Can you imagine a cottage with a disposer grinding up things or a dishwasher chugging in the background? I'd rather have a peaceful atmosphere," she says.

Master bedroom. First, she brought in light by installing lots of glass. "The day I learned I could knock most of a wall out and add my doors and windows without having

Far left: *If a friend offered old porch posts covered with years of moss, cobwebs, and dirt, most would have declined the rotting relics. But René saw them as the perfect addition to her bedroom—her bed sprouting into a four-poster with added height and sensual appeal. René gathered the flowers on a trip to San Francisco. The stunning dried selection includes delphiniums, eucalyptus, calla lilies, baby's-breath, and roses.*

Left: *René doesn't mind that a bathroom floor of used brick is less than practical. "It gives me the look I wanted."*

Below: *A backyard bench offers a secluded spot to relax.*

Sanctuary

the roof fall on my head, I was a very happy person," she says.

A four-poster bed was created by wrapping vines around porch posts. Then, she angled the bed into a corner and put a triangle-shape wooded frame at ceiling height. Flowers hanging from it may look like they dangle above her pillow, but they are safely behind it. Anything that falls will settle into the corner of the floor.

Bathroom. Again, she had a recycled window installed and a secondhand shutter became the door. Also, salvaged sink and faucets give the room more character than the standard vanity and sink.

Reading room. The walls gain immeasurably from an idea she borrowed from a studio photo she spotted in a designer's catalog. After painting walls pink, she tacked up inexpensive wood lattice painted white. The result offers color variation and an eye-catching depth.

At every turn throughout the house, René has applied her own touch without siphoning her budget dry. Results recycle notions about the high cost of living.

"As I said, with all the traveling I do, I wanted to create my own little piece of heaven right here," she says. "And I've done it. Once I walk through that door, I'm right where I want to be." □

Left: *The reading room gets an inexpensive boost from mat floor, latticework, and recycled fireplace mantel and doors.* Above: *Guest bedroom has a carved headboard from René's grandmother and a canopy from her great-grandmother.* Below: *A wooden archway is a garden triumph.*

Sanctuary

Taken with the primitive beauty of hand-hewn logs, Tom and Anne Brown joined two historic buildings to make one charming Montana home.

By Eileen Gallagher

As newlyweds, Tom and Anne Brown dreamed of building a country farmhouse with a wood frame and cedar siding. They often roamed the foothills not far from Montana's Glacier National Park looking for a spot to call their own.

Had it not been for a fateful Sunday drive 11 years ago, the couple would have built their wood-frame dream house and "been miserable," Anne admits. Instead, they ended up with an unusual log home, and a love for hand-hewn timbers.

"We were driving by and saw this frame house sitting in the middle of a cow pasture," Anne says. The siding had tumbled off one end, exposing the logs beneath it.

"We'd driven by it lots of times, but didn't realize it was log underneath," Anne says. "We had to have it, but we didn't know what we were going to do with it."

Half an hour and $500

Below: *An 1880s cabin and log granary form this home.*

Left: *Antiques and homemade reproductions fill the interior.*

CABIN
F·E·V·E·R

Produced by Peggy A. Fisher and Beverly Hawkins

later, the couple owned the circa-1880s cabin.

A self-employed carpenter, Tom was impressed with the original maker's meticulous craftsmanship. The hand-hewn logs were squared off and fitted together with dovetailed corners. "The notches fit so well," he says. "The hewing job was amazing."

As Tom and Anne hauled out knee-deep cow manure from the cabin, they needed keen vision to picture a livable abode with more than just rugged charm.

Family and friends helped Tom dismantle the structure and move it to the 4-acre property the couple bought near Columbia Falls.

"Then we had to start looking for another building," says Anne, a Montana native who returned to the Flathead Valley after living in the Midwest. It took Tom three years to locate, dismantle, and haul two more old buildings to the site. One was a granary from a homestead in nearby Somers. Scratched into one of its logs was the date 1893.

Tom fashioned ceiling beams from logs found in a barn down the road. Using a pickup, winch, and cables strung between trees, Tom set cabin and granary logs in place himself, joining them in a T-shape structure. The larch logs of the granary and the yellow pine logs of the cabin meshed beautifully.

The cabin became the living room. The granary

was transformed into a kitchen/dining area, bath, and a studio for the folk art and holiday ornament business that Anne owns with a friend.

The granary's original walls extended several feet above the first floor, creating part of a second story. Tom built the upstairs by extending the walls even higher. A dormer houses 9-year-old

Above: *Tom, Anne, and 9-year-old Cale Brown live amid pine trees and wildlife.*

Left: *The antiques come from places east. Tom built the cupboard that holds redware.*

CABIN
F E V E R

Cale's bedroom, the master bedroom, and a small space for storage. By steepening the pitch of the cabin roof, Tom was able to tuck a laundry room underneath.

Respectful of integrity, Tom gave the structure's vintage voice its full due. He chinked walls, hammered down wide-plank floors, installed pine ceilings with beams, and recycled old windows that he picked up at a yard sale and from a lumberyard.

Although finish work would take another four years to complete, the Browns moved into their historic home July 4, 1986, celebrating a little slice of American history. The rustic home's unadorned lines and simple interiors bespeak an earlier Montana life-style.

"One of the biggest things we like is the simplicity," Tom says. "When we first started, we liked the idea of a hewed-log building. Our idea grew to 'let's keep it as simple as possible and still be livable.' "

In adherence to the past, Anne sought a pared-down look inside with few and scattered furnishings. A former antiques dealer, she judiciously combined pine antiques from her collection with reproduction furniture built by Tom. Her reproduction samplers and wreaths, and dried arrangements from the herb garden, brighten the primitive interior. These touches stamp the home as unmistakably their own yet preserve the historic

character embedded within the sturdy chinked walls.

The Browns have since salvaged three more old cabins to use as outbuildings.

"It's kind of become an obsession to save the old hewn-log buildings. Here's a part of the history of the [Flathead] Valley. The few that are left are going in a hurry," Tom says. "I want to save them, and if we can't use them, let someone else." ▢

Left: *Here Anne crafts Santas for her folk art business.*

Above: *The master bedroom's Spartan furnishings blend with clean architectural lines.*

SEEDS OF GLORY

Following a lengthy Utah tradition, Shosho Zipprich draws forth a fruitful harvest from the rocky soil of the West.

Left: *Mounded perennial beds filled with peonies, columbines, irises, poppies, and more form a colorful landscape that changes continually throughout the growing season.*

Above right: *Brick and rock pathways edged with pinks, pansies, or other low-profile plants meander through the garden's many sections.*

Bottom right: *Shosho spends upward of 20 hours a week working in the garden during the spring and summer months.*

The mandate of the Mormon pioneers was clear—to coax a new Eden from the desolate land surrounding the Great Salt Lake. Few Gentiles thought they would succeed; legend has it that mountain man Jim Bridger even offered Brigham Young a thousand dollars for the first bushel of corn raised in that godforsaken place.

If Bridger, in truth, doubted the Latter-day Saints' abilities to transform the Utah wasteland, they soon proved him wrong. Relying on cooperative effort to build dams and irrigation canals, the Mormon pioneers transformed the parched terrain into a patchwork of productive green. Their orderly towns were bright with roses and flowering fruit trees, their streets lined with towering poplars—all while other Western settlements remained shackled to the six-shooter rather than led by the plow.

Today, Utah gardeners—both Mormon and non-Mormon—continue the Saints' horticultural tradition, battling drought and rocky soil, temperature extremes, and an often cruelly brief growing season to cultivate lush pockets of greenery throughout the state.

For gardener Shosho Zipprich, the rewards are well worth the long hours of weeding and watering.

"I get such a charge out

Photographs: William N. Hopkins.

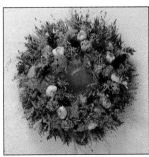

of seeing plants come up," she says. "I just love it in the spring when there's nothing, and then all of a sudden something pokes its head up. It's addictive."

When Shosho bought her house in 1977, the backyard was a plowed-over field, and the front yard, grass. Today, Shosho's lot is a succession of sculptured perennial beds, a fenced herb garden, and a neatly laid-out vegetable patch.

Surprisingly, the overall plan of the garden was not worked out in advance. "I see one section in my head, and then I do it—I want it to be reality. Then each year I make notes of the things I have to change the following year. I don't think you ever get it quite right," Shosho says.

Paths of brick or rock wind through much of the garden; the rock walkways serve a practical as well as aesthetic purpose. "When I first started the garden, the soil was about forty percent rock," Shosho explains. Though she sieved out as many rocks as she could, each spring there seemed to be just as many as before. "That's why I have those paths," she says. "I have my weeding bucket and my de-rocking bucket."

Rocks aren't the only part of the garden Shosho

makes use of. Throughout the growing season, she harvests flowers and herbs, then dries them and binds them into wreaths and floral swags, or mixes them in potpourris. All are sold through her at-home business, Wild Wood Design.

Although Shosho loves fresh flowers, she rarely picks them for bouquets.

"I'm outside most of the time, so who needs flowers in the house?" she says. "I'd rather go out with some coffee in the morning or a glass of wine in the evening and enjoy them."

Vegetables, however, she harvests with abandon. Lettuce, spinach, beets, carrots, onions, radishes, and potatoes are all well suited to the short growing season of Utah's Heber valley. In good years, cucumbers, squash, and tomatoes are, too. Some seasons, Shosho even has a bumper crop of corn.

Perhaps Jim Bridger will take note. □

Far left: A crab apple tree pruned in a basket shape is at the heart of the fenced herb garden.

Bottom: A vegetable patch Mr. McGregor would be proud of.

Below: Every corner of the large lot is under cultivation.

$\mathscr{K}$EEPER
OF THE $\mathscr{F}$LAME

Inspired by the faith of his pioneer ancestors, John Told has made the preservation of their architectural legacy his sacred mission.

$\mathscr{H}$is obsession with Mormon houses began when he was 6, not with this house but with one just down the street. "I used to make my grandmother drive me through Midway and park at the Timp Freeze ice-cream counter," John Told says. "I'd stare at the house across the way and say to myself, 'Someday I'll own that.'"

When John grew up, he moved to Hollywood. But something about that house kept calling him back to Midway, a tiny rural town in Utah's alpinelike Heber Valley.

Then, in 1982, he heard that another Midway house, designed by Mormon pioneer John Watkins (an English convert who had once been an architect for Queen Victoria), was in danger of being torn down to make way for a minimart. "I bought it on the phone," recalls John. "The next weekend I flew back to see it and thought, *'What did I do?'*"

He had imagined the house would look like his youthful passion: red brick and gingerbread and fancy porches. Instead, it was a preservationist's nightmare. The house was clumsily stuccoed and had aluminum sliding windows that were sadly out of

Above: *John Told came home to his native Utah from Hollywood, Babylon of the West.*

Opposite: *John's collection of Utah pine furniture gives his 1860s house its decorative soul.*

Near left: *Designed by English convert John Watkins, this Gothic Revival jewel has been restored to its former glory.*

Photographs: William N. Hopkins.

Right: *A Utah pine washstand, cheese cupboard, and table are typical of the practical country furniture made in many Mormon pioneer settlements.*

Top left: *A Star of David pattern, punched in tin on the doors of a comb-painted pie safe, recalls the Mormon's mission to build a New Jerusalem in the Great Basin wilderness.*

Bottom left: *The narrow, stiff-backed settee with cutout splats in John's parlor is an unusual form; John has never seen another one like it. The piece has been regrained in a bold pattern resembling crotch mahogany.*

scale. A Spanish-style wrought-iron staircase corkscrewed through the building's heart, and an extensive cinder-block addition clung to its back like a fungus.

"People thought I was crazy," he says. "And maybe I was. I had no idea what was driving me."

Determined to restore the structure to its Gothic Revival grandeur, John offered a reward in the local paper for any early pictures of the house, named Bonner Corners after its original owner. After weeks of hopeful waiting, he got a call from Bernice Bonner, the last Bonner to live there.

Looking through Bernice's box of 80-year-old pictures, John could finally visualize the hidden gem he had purchased, or at least how it had looked in 1900, 24 years after it was built. When he and two local men managed to peel back the building's imprisoning crust of stucco, it was like helping a butterfly struggle forth from its chrysalis.

With the stucco gone, however, a new challenge was revealed. Clearly visible on the original brickwork were the ghosts of porch uprights and

second-floor balconies, but no porch was shown in any pictures John had. To build a replacement, John enlarged pictures of another Watkins-designed porch, then scaled the design to the size of the Bonner house.

Once the exterior transformation was complete, John braced himself to tackle the inside of the house. Over a five-year period, he gutted and replastered all the rooms, exposed and painted the wood floors, and rebuilt the original fireplaces and stairway.

Today, the resurrected structure—an architectural marvel to passersby—is a testament to the design sophistication of the Mormon pioneers who settled Midway in the 1860s. Filled with John's extensive collection of Mormon pine furniture, it's always a popular tour stop during the town's annual Swiss Days festival.

Though the project was overwhelming at times, John found that rebuilding the Bonner house brought him a profound satisfaction. "I truly believe I was sorted out or chosen to do this," he says. "I've felt unfulfilled as a Mormon because I never went on a mission. But now I feel this *is* my mission."

Perhaps so. In 1987, John's childhood dream house—architect Watkins' personal residence just down Main Street—came on the market. John now guards two early Mormon houses from the onslaughts of the 20th century, preserving their pioneer glory for generations yet to come. □

Above: *This primitive Mormon couch was made by a Swedish convert in Pleasant Grove, Utah.*

Near left: *Lowly pine and imaginative craftsmanship are married in this Mormon-made bed, which features a bold silhouette and massive turnings.*

Far left: *In the kitchen, a dry sink with classical lines contrasts with an Eastlake-influenced flour bin/cupboard combination.*

TOIL'S RICH REWARD

More than a decade of hard work has transformed this once-dilapidated Mormon homestead into a peaceful sanctuary.

Top: *This Mormon dwelling from the late 1800s has a renewed spirit.*

Above: *Homeowner Shosho Zipprich in her garden.*

Near right: *The new kitchen, skylighted from above, is a room with a view.*

Opposite: *This elegantly simple dining room once had four layers of ceiling wallpaper.*

Finally, Shosho Zipprich can sit down and relax. The bulk of the work is over, the plaster dust vacuumed away, the paintbrushes cleaned and set aside to dry. It's a well-deserved rest that's been 14 years coming.

A Wisconsin native, one-time antiques dealer, and non-Mormon, Shosho bought her tiny brick house—built by Mormons during the late 1800s—in 1977. "I was living nearby and had taken the dog for a ride," she says. "It was a beautiful day and I bought a house." She had no idea of the epic journey she was embarking on.

Structurally, the building was sound. But "improvements" to the four-room dwelling had destroyed its simple character, and nature had staked a compelling claim.

"The first March I lived here, I walked around to the south side of the house," Shosho says. "There was a hole in the foundation, and there were about five hundred snakes curled up in there hibernating. I started looking, and in every crack in the house, there was a snake sticking out. It gave me the absolute willies."

It's a typical restoration story. Whatever job Shosho undertook, whether it was eradicating snakes or repairing the living room plaster, she got more than she bargained for.

"I started to patch a few places in the living room,

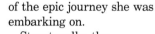

132

Photographs: William N. Hopkins.

Right: *Books, prints, baskets, and textiles add a richness of texture and pattern to this neutral-tone room. Since space was tight (the room has four doors opening into it), Shosho kept furnishings on an appropriately small scale.*

Left: *To balance the richness of the room's many antiques, Shosho sought out upholstery fabric in a putty-colored ticking stripe that gives the space an informal air.*

Below left: *The serene feeling of the house comes from its muted colors and sense of order. Clutter is minimal; each book and painting, bowl and basket is carefully placed where it can be seen and fully enjoyed.*

then pretty soon there was no plaster left on the walls," Shosho recalls. "Everything took five times longer and sixteen times more money than I'd planned. I always said, 'Oh my God, this is the worst of it,' but there was always something worse ahead."

The dining room floor was one such Pandora's box. "It had turquoise-and-chartreuse indoor-outdoor carpeting, then foam padding, then three layers of asphalt tile," she says. "I had to blowtorch it and throw boiling water on it to get it all off."

Except for the plumbing and the heating system, Shosho completed all the work herself, from gutting and replastering the rooms to marbleizing the bathroom's rebuilt woodwork. "It was trial and error," she says. "I got

wiser as I went along."

The house today, serene to both the eye and the spirit, gives no hint of the tortuous years of renovation. The living room and downstairs guest room are small but ultimately inviting, while the upstairs bedroom and sitting room serve as a comfortable private retreat. The kitchen, built in place of a dilapidated porch, is of Shosho's own design: a contemporary counterpoint to the remainder of the house.

Most of Shosho's furnishings are from New England and the Midwest, country pieces from the first half of the 19th century. "I've got this thing about new furniture," she says. "I can appreciate it in other people's homes, but I don't like it in mine. Old things have lived with other people and gone through a lot. They have history and character, their own peculiarities."

That gut-level connection with the past provided much-needed fuel during her old-house rescue mission. Less hardy souls would have given up. But like the Mormon pioneers who settled Utah long before her, Shosho's years of toil have been well rewarded. She has made herself a home, and she is here to stay. □

Above: *Shosho's under-eaves bedroom is one of two tiny rooms on the second floor.*

Left: *A short hallway joins the bedroom to a sitting room filled with some of Shosho's favorite belongings: a grain-painted English flour box, an early New England chair, and a china-head doll that was her grandfather's.*

October

The Countryside Is Her
CANVAS

Home is a masterpiece for artist Louisa McElwain and her husband, Peter Houghton

By Steve Cooper. Produced by Mary Anne Thomson

The essence of New Mexico is its rich earth. An enchant-ed canvas come to life. A colorful palette of subtle browns and delicious reds under brilliant azure skies.

Here are magnificent mesas, ar-resting arroyos, and mesmerizing moonscape mountains with haunt-ing names, such as the Sangre de Cristo—"Blood of Christ." Scat-tered across these vistas are scrub trees and such geologic blemishes as dormant volcanoes, rolling hills, and river-carved canyons.

It is a land that begs worship from the heart, boldness from the body, and attention from appreciative eyes.

"The landscape here reflects—with tremendous clarity— the chronicle of natural events that have shaped it and

Left: *Louisa McElwain's painting of the Sangre de Cristo graces the family room, which opens to the dining area and the kitchen.*

Right: *Louisa in her studio, which is separate from the main house. A section was roofed with translucent fiberglass, allowing a flood of light.*

Below: *A lawn big enough to accommodate a croquet course.*

Opening page: *Peter Houghton, Louisa McElwain, and their daughter, Maizie, outside their home.*

continue to do so," says artist Louisa McElwain, who left New England to settle in Santa Fe in 1985.

Louisa came for her art, for the landscapes, for change, and possibilities. Along the way, she met Peter Houghton, a fellow Easterner. They married, started a family, and designed a home that's like a refreshingly cool drink in this arid desert land.

Of course, this Kismet-come-true didn't begin as a highly detailed plan.

Louisa says, "It was my adventure, coming out in my pickup truck with my bicycle strapped to the front, an easel in the back, and my dog beside me."

Santa Fe promised an art enclave where a painter might earn her keep. Louisa's artistic vision found an eager, ready audience.

"My work is completely out-of-doors. All my paintings are made from start to finish on-site, which allows me to become a channel for the energy of nature," she says.

This same natural energy is reflected in the home Louisa and Peter have created.

Their dwelling is a soothing, surprising marriage of natural tones and energy efficiency. It settles into its surroundings like a broad-brimmed sombrero offering escape from the sun.

It's unmistakably New Mexico—borrowing from the familiar hacienda such details as earthy adobe walls, windows fit for a Spanish courtyard, and pergolas of boxy beams extending from the house. A strong sense of place can also be felt in the colors both inside and out, whether it is the reddish

Photographs: William N. Hopkins, Hopkins Associates.

H·E·R C·A·N·V·A·S

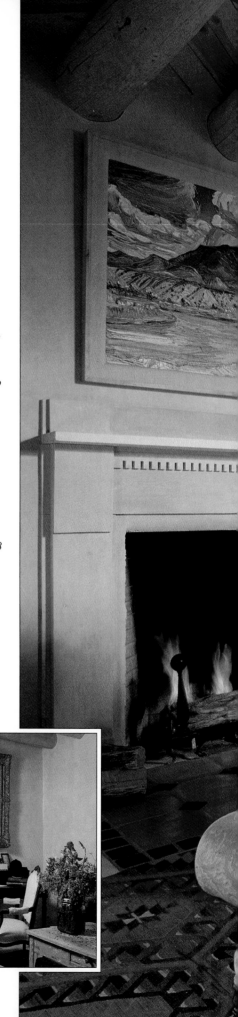

Right: *A damask sofa from Peter's grandmother and an English cherry secretary from Louisa's grandmother lend comfortable character to the living room. The coffee table was made from an old Mexican farmhouse table.*

Left: *With glass doors, the entry sets an open tone for the house.*

Below: *The height of the ceiling varies. It's 18 inches lower in the living room than in the adjacent kitchen and dining area.*

tone of dried clays, the rugged influence of bare wood, or the accents of turquoise in floor tiles.

The house carries a pitched roof, marking it as part of the northern New Mexico style. The couple decided against the flat pueblo roof commonly seen throughout the Southwest. A steep roofline not only appealed to these two Easterners, but it also avoided a pitfall endemic to flat surfaces—leaking during occasionally fierce desert rainstorms.

In addition, Peter says, "The roof gave us some overhangs to help block out summer sun." Overhangs also protect the stucco walls from exposure to drenching monsoons and winter freezing.

The house was a collaborative effort for the couple, with Louisa supplying the design concepts and Peter supervising construction.

The 3,500-square-foot house has the typical touches of a New Mexico house. These include a rounded, Southwestern-style fireplace; thick walls that allow for extraordinarily deep windowsills; adobe brick; hand-troweled, plaster interior walls; and exposed structural supports of native, rough-sawn Ponderosa pine.

There are unexpected Eastern elements here, too: dormers, boxy fireplaces, formal antique furniture, and a garden of New England plants, such as lilac and bleeding heart.

"The house doesn't adhere rigidly to any particular style, but we wanted to incorporate the best of the ones we were

H·E·R C·A·N·V·A·S

acquainted with. We've ended up with an efficient and practical house," Louisa says.

To enhance this warmth, security, and substance, Peter chose an unusual system of double walls. First he built a wall with thick adobe bricks. He surrounded this with a conventional lumber-and-insulation frame envelope.

"Because adobe has no insulation value, we would have frozen to death if that's all we used," Peter says. "But our walls are 22 inches thick in many places and work very well. It's warm in winter, all we have to do is open a window to cool it in summer, and the house is so tight you get a tremendous sense of tranquility inside."

Interior dimensions are spacious. The kitchen, dining room, and family room are a single rambling space. A strong, natural feel is maintained throughout by the use of pine and tiles for flooring, and rough-sawn beams. The understated, light tones of tinted plaster walls add finishing grace to a pleasing atmosphere.

Furnishings again reflect the East-West attitudes of Louisa and Peter. A Mexican farmhouse table sits in the same room with an English cherry

Above: *Though the kitchen is only 10 feet deep, its compact dimensions make it easy for cooking. A family friend used barn window sashes to make cabinet doors.*

Right: *The handsome stove is a Waterford, built in Ireland. Though purchased as a backup heat source, it's never been used.*

144

H·E·R C·A·N·V·A·S

Right: *A Southwestern-style fireplace warms the master bedroom. This style can be traced to Native American fire pits of the 1800s.*

Left: *The dark red pencil-post bed is draped with a French lace curtain brought from Paris by Peter's mother. Nesting in the Mennonite pine cradle are Louisa's childhood stuffed animals.*

Below: *Greenery includes local plants and hardy Eastern varieties.*

secretary from Louisa's grandmother. Spode dinnerware from Peter's grandmother mixes well with peasant pottery. One room is heated by a New Mexico-style fireplace, while in another, a Waterford stove from Ireland has been installed.

When it was complete, the house was larger than originally intended.

"The house was more overblown in scale than the little farms that inspired us," Louisa says. "But we have ended up with spaces more appropriate to our needs."

A long stone's throw from the main house, Peter also built an 800-square-foot studio for Louisa on their 7½ acres of gently rolling hills covered with piñon pine and juniper trees. It was actually the first structure built on the property. While construction of the primary residence inched toward completion, the smaller studio served as shelter for the couple.

"It's a wonderful work space. Flooded with light and great views of the mountains," Louisa says.

Many of the canvases painted here were later perched on mantels and hung on walls in the main house. Louisa's lively, colorful landscapes enrich the romantic roomscapes.

"We built a house and gardens to take advantage of the winter sun and the spectacular views . . . and created rooms appropriate to our needs, taste, and furnishings . . . with local materials and techniques," Louisa says.

The couple has accomplished much in a short time. They have successfully blended their family, home, and vocations. It's the art of living well. □

NATIVE SON

Realist painter Bob Timberlake preserves more than antiques in his 1809 barn-turned-studio. Within its chinked walls survive the cherished memories of his North Carolina heritage.

◆

By Beverly Hawkins
Produced by Candace Ord Manroe

Above: *Inspiration for Bob Timberlake's next painting lies only a few feet from his studio door.*

Right: *A settee and table meld Carolina hickory and local craftsmanship. Both are part of Bob's line of furniture and accessories.*

Photographs: William N. Hopkins, Hopkins Associates

NATIVE SON

Above: *With roots dating to the Civil War, Bob takes a keen interest in Early American memorabilia.* Opposite: *The barn's massive walls serve as a backdrop for collectibles large and small.* Below: *Cast-off wagon wheels, resting in a field of wildflowers, await an appearance in a future Timberlake painting.*

Bob Timberlake's first love affair blossomed about the time that other boys chased ponytails and pined for hot rods. Not a typical teen, Bob fell instead for the post-and-beam barn that Henry Shoaf pegged together in Davidson County, North Carolina, in 1809.

"The barn is something I have coveted since I was probably fourteen or fifteen years old, even before, maybe; I don't know," Bob says. "I had gotten my driver's license when I was fourteen, and I went hunting, canoeing, camping, and walking—all the things boys do when they're real active. This particular barn was different and unusual in the way it was constructed. It looked so durable, tough—and it stood out among the other structures in the area."

Decades passed, and a career painting images of his native state flourished, before Bob could call the barn his own. He bought and moved the structure—whose owners had defended it from destruction during the Civil War—in the mid-1980s onto 70-plus acres southeast of Lexington, North Carolina.

More than money passed hands in that fateful exchange. Along with the weathered beams came bits of Bob's North Carolina heritage, fragments of his childhood, and tales

of the way things used to be.

Hand-hewed oak logs, 50-plus-feet long, formed the barn's massive frame. They were grown in the 1600s, Bob says, and cut in the winter of 1809. Names, notches, and dates remained etched into the timbers. Boards, 48 inches wide, stretched across the floors.

It was the barn's scale and charm that Bob hoped to preserve in the studio and guesthouse he envisioned within its frame. He charged a team of craftspeople with the task of moving and renovating the barn. Piece by piece a master craftsman and his brothers transported the building to a hilltop 10 minutes away from Bob's home in town, leaving behind an old attached shed and cantilevered roof. With the barn in place on a foundation laid by a

local stonemason and his crew, the brothers fastened a 1700s log house along its backside.

"They worked on it like a piece of art," Bob says. "This structure is really one big piece of sculpture."

The barn, like every vignette that Bob has painted in his 21-year career, is a microcosm of a world he's always known and loved.

"I wanted a place that was creative, warm, and homey and surrounded by things that I loved, used, and lovingly made," Bob says. "I wanted to go back to a time of realism when people really did make things for a use and for good reasons, a time when people really chose wood for its character, its look, its durability. And the imperfections were not imperfections, but they were the beauty of the wood, and

Opposite: *Cherished sayings are etched into some of the hand-blown glass windows found throughout the studio. "Imagination is more important than knowledge," reads one of Bob's favorites.* Above: *A comfortable sitting area holds a cache of prized collectibles.* Below: *The porch was built in Adirondack style.*

they were the character and personality coming out."

The personality of the barn—like the lives of the everyday folk who appear in Bob's paintings—is as important to Bob as the structure itself. Throughout his life, Bob has attempted to preserve, for his children and grandchildren, a part of his heritage that's fading fast.

Walking into Bob's new studio is like stepping onto the canvas of another Timberlake original. The foyer floor is a mosaic of orchard stone slabs and wood. Visitors could trip over the stories and anecdotes attached to each one. The center hall paves the way to a den, office, living room, dining room, and kitchen. Two lofts overlook the main floor, and the artist's third-floor studio runs along the back.

The home showcases Bob's vast collections. These treasured pieces—antique quilts, farm buckets, enamelware pitchers, and wooden decoys—were the subjects of his paintings from the start.

To say that painting began as Bob's part-time hobby seems absurd when you realize the magnitude of his talent. Yet a mere hobby it was, in the early days, when he painted late into the night in the basement of his home, while his childhood sweetheart and wife, Kay Musgrave, tended to their three young children.

Art and architecture had long attracted Bob. At 15, he won first place in Ford Motor Company's Industrial Arts Award competition for a Pennsylvania Dutch dowry chest he built and painted. The project took 350 hours to complete.

NATIVE SON

153

Above: *A collection of canoes lines Bob's third-floor studio.* Opposite: *The bed, rug, chest of drawers, and lamp are available from various manufacturers.* Below: *"There are so many things I'd like to express and preserve in our heritage," Bob says. Sharing time with his family, including wife Kay, and grandson Rob, age 4, is a priority.*

He graduated from the University of North Carolina at Chapel Hill with a degree in architecture and set forth on a career in the family's furniture and gas

businesses. It lasted 10 years.

Bob began painting full time on New Year's Day in 1970 at the encouragement of well-known realist painter Andrew Wyeth, with whom Bob sometimes is compared. With phenomenal ease, Bob's simple style and charming manner propelled him toward success. His first two shows at the famed Hammer Galleries in New York City sold out before the previews. That successful experience opened doors for Bob, eventually taking him to London where he gave painting tips to Prince Charles. Since then, Bob has published three art books, met with presidents, designed artwork for postage stamps, and received the Albert Schweitzer Medal for Artistry.

"He's never met a stranger, so to speak," wrote the late Dr. Armand Hammer, founder of Hammer Galleries, "and most likely has never seen a sunrise or sunset that he didn't want to paint. He loves life, and it is our great joy to share in Bob's world as he embraces each new day."

Armand Hammer wasn't the only

NATIVE SON

Above: *Bob values furniture with knots, cracks, and burrows because the marks add character to a piece. "I do love textures an awful lot," he says. This willow settee and side table, for example, are deliberately rustic.*

one charmed by Bob's world. Lexington Furniture Industries of North Carolina unveiled last year The World of Bob Timberlake—more than 100 pieces of furniture inspired by Bob's personal collections. Accessories and fabrics also are available from various companies.

"Most of the pieces are from right here in my studio, or my home, or a neighbor's house," Bob says.

Many of his pieces are antiques, but others were crafted by local artisans, whose talents also have been tapped by the manufacturers. For instance, the range of products includes rugs inspired by 104-year-old weaver Sally Parnell (see *right*). There are china hutches, chests, pie safes, buffets, chairs, tables, and sideboards—some of which were designed by 83-year-old cabinetmaker

Fred Craver, who still uses many of the hand tools and techniques of the old-world masters. Clyde Gobble recently left a successful career in the insurance industry to pursue pottery. His trademark red-and-blue pieces also are highlighted in the collection.

The fact that a local company offers furniture and accessories designed and made by local people is important to Bob.

"It fell in place right in my backyard," Bob says. "These are the people I grew up with, went to school with—played with in my backyard. They're making the samples, they're running the factories, they're sanding the furniture."

In typical Timberlake style, Bob has once again created a setting where his friends and neighbors—not fame or fortune—are the focus.

"I can't tell you what a personal pride is going into all this," Bob says. "We're not kin, but we're family. We don't take heritage lightly." □

NATIVE SON

Aunt Sally and Her Rag Rugs

There are only 52 days a year—the Sundays—that "Aunt Sally" Parnell doesn't settle herself into the kitchen of her North Carolina home and weave on her 200-year-old loom. Her eyesight isn't quite the same as when her mother taught her nearly a century ago to pass the shuttle back and forth across an emerging rug. But at age 104, Sally weaves more with her heart, anyway, than with her hands and eyes.

"Sally Parnell is weaving rugs that I took my first steps on," says Bob Timberlake, who has incorporated Sally's work into his latest venture—a line of furniture, rugs, fabric, and accessories inspired by his belongings. "She's passing on that craftsmanship, that look, and that wonderful folk art into the Capel rugs we're doing."

Sally still lives in the century-old house that her father built and still embraces the simple values by which she was raised. Like Bob, and the other native craftspeople contributing to his line of furniture and accessories, Sally preserves a slice of North Carolina history.□

December

F aith sees the unseen, maintains hope against strong opposition, and perseveres. Patricia and Junior Clark are people of faith.

So when doubting Thomases expressed misgivings about their plans to erect an authentic New England saltbox on a wooded lot in the heart of Oklahoma, the Clarks wouldn't surrender their

Left: *A collection of antique cookware, including kettles, pots, and an herb grinder (on floor to right of bench), is displayed around this keeping room cooking hearth in Junior and Pat's home. Another collection, this one of Santas, is propped on the 15-foot mantel.*

Right: *The keeping-room ceiling beams were made the old-fashioned way—they were hewed with an adz.*

Opening pages: *The home was adapted from a design by Russell Swinton Oatman. The original plans are part of Oatman's Old Sturbridge Village Collection. Pat and Junior stand in the front doorway.*

🌲 🌲 🌲

hopes for a dream home to the naysayers.

"Not many people around here understood what we were trying to do, but that didn't stop us," says Pat.

So now, as visitors approach the residence during the holidays, they may feel they've arrived in New England for Christmas. Transplanted to Sooner territory is a distinctive colonial shape decked with holly wreaths, yards of ribbon, and a Christmas-red front door.

Upon entering, guests immediately notice spicy fragrances wafting through period-perfect rooms.

"The smell of spices at Christmas reminds me of the frankincense and myrrh that the Magi presented to the Christ child. I like to use them during the holidays—and they give the house a nice fragrance," she says.

The house itself recalls an earlier America and seems as authentic as a chapter from a history text, though allowance also has been made for such amenities as plumbing and electricity. The structure has three bedrooms, three baths, and more than 2,500 square feet.

Pat says, "You know how people talk about their dream house? Well, this has been mine for years and years. It is exactly what I've always wanted."

Those who know Pat aren't surprised the house has a classic American shape. She's a descendant of John and Samuel Adams and her enthusiasm for our nation's

Left: *The 7-foot dining room clock has works made of pine. The table's centerpiece includes a pineapple—a colonial symbol of hospitality.*

Top right: *With four fireplaces in their home, including this one in the dining room, the Clarks need never go cold. Beside it stands a 6-foot, 19th-century feather tree. Staffordshire figurines are displayed in the wall recess.*

Bottom right: *Miniature celluloid animals enliven a Christmas scene atop an antique German dower chest.*

🌲 🌲 🌲

history blossomed during her school days. Now she feeds her passion by collecting Americana.

Pat says, "Collecting is a way of life for us. We're interested in preserving our American heritage, and Junior and I make it a joint effort. That's the fun of it."

As diligently as they've collected objects, the Clarks also have collected informa-tion. During their frequent trips to museums, Junior and Pat have gained in-sights into colonial-era home life. Fortunately, Ju-nior works for a major air-line, allowing for the couple's extensive travel.

As their antiques collec-tion grew with each trip, the Clarks began to envision a new home, one that would provide an appropriate en-vironment for display. A saltbox seemed a proper choice for such pieces as their gateleg table, a hired-man's rope bed, banister-back chairs, a Bible box,

163

Right: In the parlor, Canton ware and delftware fill a corner cupboard. The keeping room can be seen through the open door.

Top left: The kitchen cabinets were designed to blend with the home's historical theme but still offer modern convenience. Pat made the apple-cone tree decoration on the table.

Bottom left: The Clarks bought this Nativity set the first year they were married. It remains a favorite of the couple and their now-grown children, Butch and Pam.

🎄 🎄 🎄

a chandelier from a Quaker meetinghouse, and other time-honored furnishings.

"We didn't want a museum. But we did want a place that would reflect our interest in American history and be a logical home for our collections," Pat says.

Having decided what they were going to build, the Clarks began their search for appropriate materials. To find pine in the width and quality they sought, they traveled 300 miles to a two-man sawmill in western Arkansas hill country. They picked through stacks of fresh-cut timber to select their lumber and returned in six months to haul the dried planks home. Once they got it home, Junior unloaded all 8,000 pounds himself.

Wisely, the Clarks hired help to gather Arkansas River rocks that would cover part of the structure. Tons of stone caked with moss and algae were used to give the exterior an aged appearance.

Having carefully selected rock and lumber, the couple also gave close attention to the windows. Gracing exterior walls are 34 windows, each with two dozen panes. Because the German-made glass is hand-blown, surfaces have wavy imperfections, which blur the view.

"We could have just gone out and bought new

Left: *Elegant panel-ing around the fire-place and boxed ceiling beams lend a sense of formality to the Clarks' mas-ter bedroom. The table where Santa has left his pipe is an early shoe-foot hutch table.*

Top right: *A collec-tion of stuffed ani-mals and playful figures gathers atop the rope bed in a whimsically deco-rated extra bed-room. A pair of horsehair-filled boxing gloves hangs over the footboard.*

Bottom right: *When Pam was young, she and Pat decorated this English dollhouse according to the season.*

🌲 🌲 🌲

windows that would be absolutely clear," Pat says. "I'm sure they'd perform better. But when you look out these windows, it gives you the sense that you're really in an old house. That's what we were after."

Another authentic element the Clarks chose is simple pine-plank flooring. Pine is a softwood prone to marring, splitting, and gouging. However, homeowners valuing historical accuracy more than pristine performance accept this wood species' inherent inadequacies.

Because pine also has a tendency to cup, or curl, Junior and carpenter Tom Little might have ended up with a roller-coasterlike floor. To prevent this, two saw rips were made running the full length and half the depth of each board's underside. After two years, the floor remains perfectly flat.

"Pine floors really aren't difficult to live with and they lend a character other kinds of floors can't," Pat says.

All these details—the pine floors, authentic glass, hand-picked lumber, and furnishings—are faithful to the colonial roots of the ar-chitecture. The home is also testimony to the Clarks' deeply held religious faith.

Pat says, "Ultimately, as much as we love this house, we know our possessions aren't what this life is about. So we accept this house as a gift of the Lord . . . and feel very blessed." □

New England Born and Bred

High on a hill to the west of Woodbury, Connecticut, a sturdy saltbox, sheathed in gray clapboards, rises like a phantom from the icy mist. So timeless are its lines that it might be mistaken for one of the town's earliest dwellings. In truth, it is a reconstruction built from two old barns. But the family who lives here *is* one of the town's earliest; their history in Woodbury stretches back to the mid-1600s.

With such a venerable family tree, one might expect the Drakeleys to show a bit of Yankee reserve. But, when Bill and Joyce Drakeley, their five children and their spouses, and their two grandchildren (along with the Drakeleys' three dogs and three cats) gather to celebrate the Christmas season, the house reverberates with raucus good cheer.

To set the stage for the annual Christmas gathering, Joyce enlists the aid of her

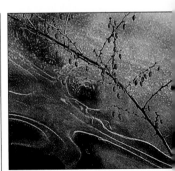

Left: *Two antique barns provided the structure for this classic house.* Top: *Hand-forged rosehead nails punctuate the building's clapboards.*

New England
Born and Bred

daughter-in-law Chris Drakeley, who has a year-round business in Woodbury making dried floral arrangements and wreaths. This year, Chris and Joyce decked the Drakeleys' living area with garlands of boxwood decorated with pink pepperberry bunches and evergreen festoons trimmed with delicate dried hydrangeas and roses. They dressed the Christmas tree, cut at the local tree farm, with china and glass ornaments, rosebud pomanders, and ribbons, along with baby's breath and strands of gleaming pearls.

For the Drakeleys' bedroom and bedroom sitting area, Chris fashioned rich swags and lunettes of salal, hydrangeas, wild rose hips, dried roses, and gold ribbon. The bedroom tree is laden with ornaments from Christmases past, including many made by the Drakeley kids when they were in elementary school. Although it lacks the elegance of its living room counterpart, this tree—a sort of three-dimensional scrapbook of their family history—is the Drakeleys' favorite.

Not surprisingly, Bill and Joyce and their children have a stake in preserving Woodbury's heritage along with their family history. "It's different knowing your family has

New England Born and Bred

Above: *Daughter-in-law Chris Drakeley made this sugared fruit decoration by brushing fresh fruit with beaten egg white, then rolling the pieces in sugar.* Right: *The post-and-beam barns the Drakeleys used for the basic structure of the house allowed them to keep the spaces open and airy, far different in feeling from most vintage homes. The row of Palladian windows provides an unimpeded view of the valley Bill's family has called home for more than three centuries.*

been part of a town from the beginning," says Bill, a seventh generation Woodbury native.

Together, the Drakeleys have restored a handful of historic buildings in Woodbury. Spurred on by their success with original structures, they decided to tackle building their own home in 1986.

The idea of using old barns for the project developed quite by chance. "We were sitting on our car bumper waiting for a guy to sell us an old Dutch barn, when we noticed two other barns," says Joyce. "I just knew we could put the two together and make a house."

The project took the family three years to complete. Bill did all of the planning; then he, his sons, and four local carpenters (also descendants of original Woodbury settlers) erected the massive structure. Only the sketchiest plans were outlined ahead of time.

"When Bill went to buy lumber for a door, the merchant requested the building plans," Joyce says. "Bill pulled out a little piece of paper and gave it to him. That's all there was."

Once the building was solidly in place, the Drakeleys tackled the interiors. The barns had been quite suitable for their original four-footed residents, but Bill and Joyce wanted more

New England Born and Bred

Above: *Walls finished in white plaster accentuate the massive chestnut and pine beams left visible throughout the house. The tester bed was made by decoy carver Richard Morgan, a Woodbury resident.*
Right: *The Drakeleys' bedroom was designed with space for this sitting area and fireplace, as well as an office loft.*

genteel surroundings. First, they salvaged a dilapidated saltbox and reused its chestnut floorboards, stone fireplaces, and massive lintel. Vintage doors and other elements were collected over a four-year period.

On the exterior, Bill, his sons, and the carpenters attached the clapboards with rosehead nails, pounded into hand-drilled holes. "I thought I'd go bankrupt on nails," says Bill.

The finished house is of heirloom quality, enriched by the patina of age yet blessed with modern comforts. Palladian windows soar upward in the living room and dining area, opening the heart of the house to the outdoors. The rooms are larger and more open than in typical period houses due to their barn beginnings, affording plenty of elbowroom for holiday gatherings. Even the furnishings—a comfortable combination of New England antiques, overstuffed sofas, and wingback chairs—stand up well amidst the happy tumult of the holidays.

"This is not a delicate house," Joyce says. Delicate would hardly do. The Drakeleys expect their house as well as their family to be a part of Woodbury—and the town's festive Christmas celebrations—for many generations yet to come. □

A Gathering Of Greens

Above: Chris snips some evergreens with husband Bill Drakeley, Jr., and their son, Billy. Right: Nestled in Woodbury's Hollow, the Drakeleys' house dates to the early 1800s. Topiary reindeer forage in the fresh snow; these shaggy creatures were made by Bill's aunt.

The branches are like clay in Chris Drakeley's hands. She cajoles them into shape, binding them with wire and sculpting them with clippers, her gloved fingers moving in an unbroken rhythm. She works swiftly, sure of the outcome, undaunted by unruly twigs, short stems, and broken boughs. She is master of her materials—an artist with greens and dried flowers.

Christmas is Chris's busiest season, when she twines hundreds of pounds of greenery and dried plant material into festive wreaths, swags, and garlands to decorate Woodbury, Connecticut's, homes. Some of her projects are humble at heart and hardy enough to withstand the winter weather: juniper wreaths dressed with raffia bows or evergreen swags bundled with red ribbon and cinnamon sticks. Others are elegant and for inside decoration only: crescents of dried roses and larkspur

A Gathering
Of Greens

Above: *The Drakeleys'*
Christmas tree is laden
with nature's bounty:
exotic pomegranates,
wild grapevines, and
clove and cranberry
pomanders.
Right: *When the house*
was renovated, the
Drakeley family opened
this originally low-
ceilinged room to the
rafters. Out of view to
the upper right is a cozy
loft bedroom, reached by
a stairway in Chris's
showroom.

bound with gossamer ribbon, or tiny topiaries
of fragrant rosebuds set in moss-filled pots.

Chris and Bill Drakeley's own home is ample
evidence of Chris's handiwork. No matter what
the season, colorful arrangements of herbs and
dried flowers, from laurel wreaths and bundles
of lavender to circlets of dried marigolds, hang
throughout the small house—a one-time silver-
smith's shop restored by Bill's family.

For the holidays, Chris adds even more em-
bellishments, including a fresh-cut tree laden
with handmade ornaments. Clove-studded ap-
ples, rosebud pomanders, and cranberry balls
hang like exotic fruit from every bough, while
ropes of grapevine and artemisia twine
through the branches like woodland creepers
around a tree trunk.

Tin icicles (from the local blacksmith) and
snowflakes cut from can lids sparkle amid the
multicolored tree lights. To add the scent of
Christmas to the air, Chris hangs ornaments
cut and baked from a spicy mixture of cinnamon, applesauce, and white glue.

Walks through the woods begin the holiday
season, as Chris gathers wild rose hips, pine-
cones, and a variety of greens for her arrangements. She orders some items by mail, from

A Gathering
Of Greens

Above: *Ropes of artemisia and cranberries, glistening with icicles, wrap the loft stairway banister.*
Top: *Chris does much of her work on this kitchen table, while Billy watches from his high chair.*
Right: *A bountiful harvest fills Chris's at-home showroom.*

miniature pomegranates (for Christmas tree ornaments) to plastic foam balls (for topiaries and pomanders). Other materials she grows herself during the summer months: lavender, lamb's ears, wormwood, artemisia, and sage. "I love being out-of-doors," she says.

Chris began her home-based business, called Herbal Classics, two years ago when son Billy was born. She already had the basic skills for the job; she had learned the art of flower arranging at a nearby vocational agricultural high school and had practiced it in summer jobs during college.

At-home work, however, required some adjustment. The tight quarters of the Drakeleys' house and the hard-to-contain nature of Chris's craft mean the floor often is carpeted with clippings, the halls blocked by buckets of dried artemisia, and the tables piled with completed wreaths and arrangements.

"I love it and I hate it," Bill says, laughing. "Chris makes everything look great, but I have to vacuum all the rugs."

The Drakeleys agree, however, that the result is well worth the inconveniences. "Now I get paid to stay home with Billy. You can't beat that," Chris says. □

HOLIDAY HILL

*This is always a special season at the home of
Joe and Gloria Sewell as they enjoy a warm country Christmas
with family and friends.*

*By Steve Cooper
Produced by Ruth Reiter*

When Joe and Gloria Sewell's three daughters were youngsters, family tradition dictated Gloria make a cherry pie each Christmas.

"We'd stick candles all over it and have the girls sing happy birthday to Jesus," Gloria says.

As her daughters—Troy, Jodi, and Shannon—grew and left home, however, the family's ritual faded into memory. Until this year, that is.

"With the birth of our first grandchild this year [daughter Shannon and her husband, Lamont Machamer, are expecting a child], this will be a very special Christmas for us," says Gloria. "We'll have our Christmas pie with candles for the first time in years and start this child off right."

It helps, of course, if these family memories take root in rooms where a loving ambience has been developed with care. The Sewells' grandchild will be blessed in this respect. Joe, a developer, built the house, and Gloria's decorative talents added a gracious, down-home atmosphere.

Perched on a Canton, Georgia, hilltop, the house settles into its site like the queen of the Twelfth Night ball. The facade is distinctively

Photographs: Mike Moreland.

Left: *A 14-foot Christmas tree rises in the entryway of Joe and Gloria Sewell's Georgia home. Most of the ornaments are handmade—some of them years ago by the couple's daughters when they were young and others by family friends. The stairwell light was handcrafted from an old beam.*

Opposite: *Joe and daughters Jodi (at reins) and Shannon look on as Gloria (left) and daughter Troy load a neighbor's wagon with Christmas greenery.*

Southern—the home wears a tiara of three dormers and a skirt of wraparound porches. From this throne, one can appreciate majestic views of surrounding, wooded hills.

Behind the main house is an 1840 chestnut log cabin, which was featured in *Country Home®* in August 1990. Gloria opens the cabin to thousands of visitors, mostly schoolchildren, for her historical tours and craft demonstrations.

The four-bedroom home's floor plan is open, welcoming, and designed for entertaining. No walls obstruct movement in the primary living area, composed of a great-room, kitchen, and breakfast room.

Gloria begins decorating for Christmas by early November. Within a few weeks, a steady stream of family friends are stopping by to cheer the day. Visiting children take particular delight in Gloria's seasonal vignettes created with toys, bears, and Santas. They enjoy whimsical scenes of bears taking tea or delivering Christmas trees.

Gloria's stenciling is an appealing, elegant feature of the formal dining room. Here, the family gathers for their annual Christmas dinner of ham, smoked turkey, October beans,

Above: *Gloria is at the kitchen cooking hearth, which also is pictured* opposite. *It's only a few steps from modern appliances.*
Below: *Teddy and family enjoy a tea party.*

*H*OLIDAY HILL

185

and other favorites. Joe and Gloria also host their extended family each year the weekend before Christmas.

The home's country feel, underscored by generous use of pine and brick, is the perfect backdrop for the couple's quintessential Southern hospitality. Wherever wood has been applied, such as on the great-room mantel or the stairway near the entrance, the design demonstrates elegance and simplicity. The design creates a natural setting for Gloria's various collections, including her Cherokee baskets, red Christmas quilts, and regional furniture.

As with any major project brought to fruition, the Sewells' hilltop home was a successful marriage of a clear vision and careful planning.

"We'd always wanted a new home with an old, country feel," says Gloria. "A place that looked like it had been around for a few years, but without all the headaches and work of an old house. This house has given us exactly what we wanted."

Long before the first spade of dirt was overturned, the couple began collecting ideas from magazines and books. Gloria created a must-have list and another list with elements she viewed as negotiable.

Left: The great-room's fireplace mantel contrasts richness of design with simplicity of materials.
Above: Gloria's stenciling gives dining room walls a flourish.
Below: Mr. Bear delivers Christmas trees.

HOLIDAY HILL

Opposite: *For the holidays, Gloria gives the master bedroom a festive touch with her Mr. and Mrs. Claus figures. Here, as in each of her rooms, greenery adds natural color and texture.*
Above: *Long before they built the house, Gloria bought this romantic clawfoot tub and pedestal sink. "I knew I'd have a house for them eventually, and I finally did," she says.*
Right: *This is one of three upstairs bedrooms. For Christmas, Gloria decorates the dollhouse, which she built when Jodi was 5, with a miniature tree and delightful lights.*

"Topping my 'must' list was a kitchen cooking hearth," Gloria says.

Her interest was sparked years ago when a winter power failure forced her to prepare dinner over burning logs. But that also led to her sympathetic realization that "pioneer women must have spent all their time cooking," she says.

Because it's such an intense and arduous task, Gloria limits hearth cooking to an occasional meal. But never on Christmas. "My first attempt was my last," she says.

High on Joe's list were porches. "The view across the creek and the countryside is very relaxing at the end of the day," he says.

Both this view and the house are so attractive that the Sewells have hosted public Christmas tours for the community. Two years ago, 2,000 people visited their home for a Yuletide perusal.

Gloria says, "I love the house more at Christmas than any other time of year because of the pleasure it brings to others. Isn't that what a home is all about?" □

HOLIDAY HILL

Index